AMERICAN
REDWARE

HENRY HOLT AND COMPANY

New York

AMERICAN REDWARE

William C. Ketchum, Jr.

Published by Henry Holt and Company, Inc.,
115 West 18th Street, New York, New York 10011.
Published in Canada by Fitzhenry & Whiteside Limited,
195 Allstate Parkway, Markham, Ontario L3R 4T8.

Library of Congress Cataloging-in-Publication Data
Ketchum, William C., 1931–
American redware / William C. Ketchum, Jr.
p. cm.
Includes bibliographical references.
ISBN 0-8050-1262-1 (alk. paper)
1. Redware—United States. I. Title.
NK4283.K4   1991
738.3'0973—dc20   90-34516
                                                   CIP

Henry Holt books are available at special discounts for bulk
purchases for sales promotions, premiums, fund-raising,
or educational use. Special editions or book excerpts
can also be created to specification.
For details contact:
Special Sales Director, Henry Holt and Company, Inc.,
115 West 18th Street, New York, New York 10011.

First Edition

DESIGNED BY LUCY ALBANESE

Printed in the United States of America
Recognizing the importance of preserving the written word,
Henry Holt and Company, Inc., by policy, prints all of its
first editions on acid-free paper.∞

1 3 5 7 9 10 8 6 4 2

CONTENTS

ACKNOWLEDGMENTS

No book of any merit is ever written without the collaboration and assistance of others. In this case I particularly wish to thank my editor, Tracy Bernstein, whose wise advice and unflapability in the face of the various crises that attend the putting together of a manuscript have made a rough road smooth; my agent, Anne Edelstein, and Esto Photographics, which provided the illustrations for the text.

INTRODUCTION

AT A TIME when folk art in general is held in high esteem, it seems particularly appropriate to examine the work of those American craftsmen who labored in clay, turning out vessels that although essentially utilitarian ofttimes reached the level of plastic art. While not entering into the tedious and self-serving arguments between the art historians and anthropologists as to what constitutes "folk art," any sensitive person will quickly see that, either in form or decoration, some American redware equals in quality the finest paintings, sculpture, furniture, and metalwork produced in this country.

It is the purpose of this book to provide the ceramics collector with a general guide to the redware made throughout the United States from the seventeenth to the early twentieth centuries. Since the common brick-red firing clay from which redware takes its name is found almost everywhere, these potters worked in many areas. However, our westward expansion did not reach very far until late in the nineteenth century, when other more practical materials such as stoneware, tin, and glass were replacing redware. As a consequence, most examples are from the eastern, southern, or midwestern states.

That is not all that is available, though; states such as Arkansas, Texas, Colorado, Utah, and California can provide the enthusiast with interesting additions to his collection. It just requires a bit more searching.

Upon finding a choice piece, most collectors are curious as to who made it, and where and when. Sadly enough, this information is usually unknown. Redware was seldom marked in any way by its maker, and similar forms were made over a long period of time and in many different areas. For instance, the common bean pot has been produced since the seventeenth century and is still being made today. An example turned out by a Massachusetts craftsman in 1680 differs little from one made in Missouri two hundred years later.

Marked redware, therefore, takes on added importance for the collector. Recognizing this, we have compiled the most complete listing of American redware manufacturers' marks ever assembled. It should serve both as a form of identification and as a guide for the increasing number of individuals who choose to collect only marked ware.

The reader will note also that among the illustrations are many unmarked pieces and that those are attributed to specific states or areas. While such attributions are done on the basis of current knowledge, they should always be viewed conservatively. As mentioned previously, potters in different communities produced similar forms and decorations, often over a long period of time. A potter moving from job to job carried with him his technique and his tools, such as punches and molds.

Often dealers, eager to enhance the value of an otherwise mundane piece by convincing a customer that it was produced by John Bell or some other well-known craftsman, will be free with attributions that should be considered most carefully. Unless a piece is marked, has a reliable provenance, or is nearly identical to a marked example or to sherds excavated at a pottery site, claims as to its origin are suspect.

The illustrations have been chosen to show the great variety of forms produced by the American redware potters. Since most prior books in this field and the major institutional collections tend to focus on pieces such as plates and large storage vessels that allow a broad surface for decoration, they create the impression that craftsmen made only a few different items. Nothing could be further from the truth. There are literally dozens of different forms, and a collection need not be limited to pie plates, platters, and jugs.

Moreover, I have chosen to illustrate pieces that are generally available to the collector and may still be purchased at prices within the means of most enthusiasts. A book dedicated only to examples from the collections of major museums has little relevance for the average collector who can seldom hope to own such pieces. With the exception of some examples with sgraffito and slip decoration that have been included to provide a complete picture of the field, there is nothing here beyond the average collector's reach.

AMERICAN
REDWARE

1

REDWARE POTTERY MANUFACTURE

THE ART AND CRAFT of the redware potter is nowhere better illustrated than in *Ugetsu*, the Japanese director Mizoguchi's great drama of the feudal age. The movie opens with two potters carefully preparing a kiln for baking. The ware is stacked, the fires are lit; then, out of nowhere, waves of samurai combatants, whose feuds and allegiance mean nothing to the simple craftsmen, rush down upon the remote village. All is swept away. The potters flee. Days later they return. The deserted town is in ruins, but the unopened kiln still stands. They pull aside the bricks that block the entrance, revealing the finest ware they had ever produced!

Though rarely so dramatic, every redware potter's efforts were fraught with equal uncertainty. No two kiln loads were ever the same, and much that we regard today as a reflection of the craftsman's skill is actually the result of uncontrollable factors—clay content, glaze variations, firing temperature, even the time of the year.

Yet the American craftsman attempted to regulate all these factors, just as his predecessors had for countless generations. Little that the colonial potter did was new or unique to these shores. The ways he shaped his wares, decorated them, and finally fired them were traditional.

Characteristically, a redware shop was run by one or a few men, often related. If more hands were needed, as when clay was dug or a kiln fired, neighbors, wives, and children shared the tasks. The business was seldom operated on a full-time basis. There was at least subsistence farming, and often the potter would also tend sheep and cattle, prune his orchards, and hire out as a day laborer when things got slow. His local reputation seldom depended upon his skills as an artisan. Indeed, when Alvin Wilcox of West Bloomfield, one of the most important New York State potters, died in 1862, the *Rural New Yorker* noted only that "a good and useful man has departed."

Redware was always inexpensive, so costs,

1

particularly of raw materials, had to be low. Craftsmen settled where suitable clay had been exposed along stream banks or road cuts, and where extensive woodlands assured a fuel supply. Customers were another necessity, and most nineteenth-century American redware potteries were built either beside the turnpikes that carried settlers west or in the midst of rapidly developing farmlands.

CLAY PREPARATION

Clay, the key to success, was excavated in spring or fall and was brought by wagon to the shop where it was stored in a cellar or hole to "season" for several months. As dug, the earth was coarse in texture and filled with sand, pebbles, and vegetation. After having been exposed to the weather for a suitable period, which would enhance its plasticity, it was refined. First, the lumps of raw clay were placed in a shallow, circular pit that had been lined with wood or stone. A long wooden paddle that revolved on a shaft extended into this depression, crushing and grinding the raw earth into a single semi-fluid mass. Motive power for this device might be human, or come from water or even steam, as in the later more advanced shops; but characteristically, it was driven by a horse or mule who spent his day plodding in a circle about the mill, often bearing the additional burden of neighborhood children grateful for their improvised merry-go-round. It is said that animals employed in this manner invariably grazed in a circle when let out to pasture.

Foreign bodies such as pebbles, grit, or twigs (which if allowed to remain in the soil until firing would "explode," producing unsightly holes and scars) were removed by washing and screening the clay, which involved flooding it with water and then forcing the creamy mixture (*slip*), by means of a hand press called a *jack*, through a series of progressively finer mesh screens into a large vat where it was allowed to stand and drain.

Once dry, the clay was cut into oblong blocks and stored until needed, at which point it was run through a *pug mill*, which was a cylindrical vat with a spiral-shaped central shaft like that of a meat grinder. Clay poured into the top of this device emerged from the bottom thoroughly mixed and ready for use. Smaller pug mills were hand-driven, while larger ones utilized horsepower.

The long log-shaped pieces of clay, termed *bolts*, which were extruded from the pug mill, were cut into uniform cubes or cylinders measured by weight or by eye to be sufficient for the manufacture of specific objects, such as jugs, pitchers, and bowls.

MAKING THE WARE

Potter's clay, when prepared this way, was of a uniform consistency and plasticity. It could be shaped in one of several ways. Hand forming or modeling is the most ancient method of manufacture and one familiar to every schoolchild.

The clay is pinched and pulled into shape, or pressed into slabs that may then be joined to form a hollow vessel, or rolled into long "ropes" that can be coiled into a basketlike form. Native Americans favored coiling, but modeling in general was seldom employed by white potters. A notable exception, however, was the manufacture of small toys and whistles, particularly in Pennsylvania and Virginia.

The great majority of American redware was produced on the potter's wheel. In its most elementary form, the wheel consisted of two horizontally mounted wooden disks joined by a vertical shaft. Although later water-powered and today electrified, earlier wheels were driven by the potter who rhythmically kicked a treadle attached to the lower shaft (hence the term *kick wheel*), causing the disks to rotate.

Unglazed exteriors of two nineteenth-century redware milk pans. Clearly visible are the ridges left by the potters' fingers and tools as they turned the vessels.

The potter centered a lump of clay on the upper disk and, aided by centrifugal force as it spun, raised and shaped the mass into a hollow vessel. Handles and spouts were formed separately and then attached to the piece. Other than the potter's wheel, few tools were required. Various wooden ribs or smoothers were used to remove the mark of the potter's fingers and to shape necks and rims. A wet sponge gave a final polish and a piece of wire was used to cut the base of the finished vessel from the wheel.

While the great majority of early American redware is wheel-formed, we will find pieces made in other ways. Pie plates and oblong or oval platters were often produced by a process called *drape molding*. A ball of clay was pounded flat, then cut into the desired shape and draped over a wooden, clay, or plaster form. After the clay slab (usually referred to as a *bat*) had taken

the shape of the form and dried sufficiently to be handled, the outside or back would be smoothed with a wet sponge, the edges trimmed, and the piece lifted off the mold and set aside for decoration and eventual firing. Drape molding was almost universal, being utilized in the making of pie plates from Maine to Utah.

A related process, *press molding*, involved the forcing of clay into a mold made in two or three sections so it could be taken apart. Once the clay

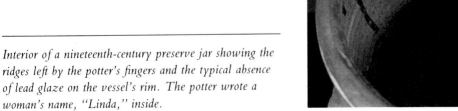

Interior of a nineteenth-century preserve jar showing the ridges left by the potter's fingers and the typical absence of lead glaze on the vessel's rim. The potter wrote a woman's name, "Linda," inside.

Not all redware plates were decorated. The large pie plate is from New Jersey, c. 1860–90, and the small eating plate is from Pennsylvania, c. 1840–70. Both are typical of the plain dishes in common use during the nineteenth century.

Mold-formed manganese-glazed redware teapot attributed to John Mann of Rahway, N.J., c. 1830–50. These classical teapots were modeled on English forms.

had dried, the mold was disassembled and the piece removed. Such a form might have decorative designs either cut into its surface or raised above it, and these would be mirrored on the surface of the clay body. Press-molded redware is not particularly common. Most examples can be traced to kilns in Virginia, North Carolina, or Pennsylvania. But, since the molds were small and usually owned by individual potters, similar ware may appear wherever the craftsmen wandered. Examples have been traced to potteries in Vermont, New York, Ohio, and Illinois, for example.

Slip casting, the most sophisticated method of molding pottery, was not customarily employed by redware makers, perhaps because they could not afford or obtain proper molds or lacked the refined clay body necessary to achieve a satisfactory result. Nevertheless, examples, particularly from Vermont, Pennsylvania, and North Carolina, are known.

In slip casting, liquid clay or slip is poured into a plaster or unbaked clay mold that is made

Two covered sugar bowls or preserve jars with incised designs and slip decoration; both attributed to David Mandeville, Orange County, N.Y., c. 1830–40. Note the unusual "rope twist" handles.

in two or three hinged sections. As the water in the slip is absorbed by the mold, a thin layer of clay adheres to the sides of the form. The excess slip is then poured out and the clay body is allowed to dry and harden before the mold is opened for its removal. Slip-cast redware may be distinguished from press-molded examples by its hollow, thin-walled body.

DECORATION

The semisoft body, referred to as *green ware*, of a recently formed piece of pottery could be decorated in a variety of ways. It is important, though, to emphasize that the vast majority of American redware was not decorated at all. It was simply given a protective, waterproof glaze and fired. Decoration took time and, in some instances, money. Neither the potter nor his customers expected it on what was essentially utilitarian ware. Collector interest in elaborate examples, usually made as gifts or on special

order, has created a false impression of the role of decoration in this field.

Nevertheless, the potter with requisite skill and incentive could command a variety of decorative techniques. Some of these involved glaz-

Molded redware inkwell or inkstand, New England, c. 1830–50. These more elaborate wells were customarily referred to as stands. The form of this one mimics an early-nineteenth-century mold-blown glass example.

ing, which is discussed below; others related to the unfired clay body. While the piece was still on the wheel, the craftsman might hold an awl or even a sharp stick against its side as it slowly revolved, incising straight or wavy lines around its circumference. Or, if more artistic, he might scratch a simple flower, bird, or human figure on it—a design that might later be filled in with a colored slip glaze.

Specially made metal punches could impress rosettes, stars, or diamonds on the surface; and a *coggle wheel* (which was a small disk attached to a handle and carved in decorative motifs) could be rolled on the surface of the pot, leaving a series of impressions, such as flowers, berries, leaves, or even tiny fish.

Pennsylvania potters were especially likely to cut away portions of a piece (most often sugar bowls or tobacco jars) in decorative patterns to create pierced designs similar to those found on early silver; while in Virginia and among the Moravians of North Carolina, decoration often took the form of *sprigging*, or the application to a vessel of small press-molded or hand-shaped elements such as flowers, leaves, and even human or mythological heads and figures.

More elaborate examples, often designed as presentation pieces or as tests of an apprentice's skill, might incorporate several of these decorative techniques, as in the famous Pennsylvania sgraffito ware that combined incised decoration with the use of colored slip glazes.

GLAZING

Pottery glazes have the same purpose as the shellac or lacquer coatings given a piece of wooden furniture. Whatever their composition, they are intended to achieve several goals: to strengthen and seal the object, to give it a glasslike surface, and to decorate it.

Because baked redware is relatively soft and porous, the purpose of sealing is most impor-

A redware milk pan, lead-glazed on the interior and attributed to New England, c. 1830–60. At 16 inches in diameter, this is a medium-size pan. Some measured 24 inches across.

tant. Liquids leak or "sweat" out over time, rendering unglazed vessels impractical except as flowerpots, terra-cotta architectural ornaments, and watercoolers (where the sweating has a use in keeping the liquid contents cool).

Most American redware potters employed a basic glaze of lead and silica, which was discovered in the Near East around 1000 B.C. Used in a combination of three parts red lead, one part clay, and one part sand or silica in a watery solution called slip, this glaze fired to a clear glasslike finish through which the natural body color of the clay might be seen.

These elements were prepared by grinding them in a *glaze mill* or potter's quern that consisted of two heavy stones, the upper of which was smaller and fit loosely within the lower. As the upper stone was turned, the materials were ground against the lower stone until the finely pulverized mixture passed out a hole in the base of the mill. When mixed with water, it was then ready for use.

Grinding glazes was a tiring and tedious chore

A group of typical redware pots glazed only on the interior. Left, an apple-butter container; *rear,* a form often termed a lard pot, *and* front, a bean pot without handles. *All are from the northeastern United States, c. 1850–1900.*

and one that was often assigned to children. In an interview many years ago, the daughter of the mid-nineteenth-century potter Carl Mehwaldt of Bergholz, New York, described her part in the operation:

We children helped to grind the lead for the glaze. There was a large stone in one corner of the workroom. From the ceiling a pole was suspended, with a flat stone on the end of it, and this pole had to be kept going round and round in order to grind the lead in the tub.

My brother and I would stand on chairs and take hold of the handles and get it round and round. We would count 100 and then rest. How our arms used to ache! I can imagine I feel it in my shoulders yet, I was that tired. (Ada Walker Cammehl, "Mehwaldt, a Pioneer American Potter," *The Magazine Antiques*, September 1922)

Unfired vessels that had been allowed to stand on shelves in a cool, dry shed until in the proper *leather-hard* state were glazed by being dipped into a pot of glazing solution, or by having glaze poured in or painted on. In all cases, the bottoms and sometimes the rims were left unfinished because the ware was stacked when fired, and separate pieces would fuse or bond together where glazed areas came into contact.

The lasting popularity of lead glaze (it is still used in some countries) reflects its efficiency and inexpensiveness. However, the glaze solution had one serious problem: it was poisonous! As far back as 1785, *The Pennsylvania Mercury* warned its readers that

> . . . even when it [lead glazing] is firm enough, so as not to scale off, it is yet imperceptibly eaten away by every acid matter, and mixing with the drinks and meats of the people, becomes a slow but sure poison, chiefly affecting the nerves, that enfeebles the constitution, and produces paleness, tremors, gripes, palsies. . . .

Hardly a recommendation for ware used at that time by probably 90 percent of the American people!

Potters in the southern states also utilized two other finishes for redware, both of which were nonpoisonous and more often employed on stoneware. The first of these was an alkaline glaze made from wood ash, clay, and sand. Depending upon the ingredients, firing, and other factors, this shiny, transparent glaze may range in color from off-white to dark brown, with even some shades of yellow, green, and blue.

A second choice was *Albany slip*, a glaze prepared from a natural clay body found near Albany, New York, and in various other places throughout the United States. Mixed with water to form a slip, this clay produced a smooth and lustrous brown finish after firing. Albany slip was also sometimes used on northern redware; I have seen marked examples from Cornwall, New York, and Harrisburg, Pennsylvania, but it must be accounted rare above the Mason-Dixon line.

DECORATIVE GLAZES

While a clear lead glaze was employed by most potters most of the time, there were those who chose color. By adding coloring agents to the mixture, it was possible to create brilliant hues. The three basic colorants were iron oxide, copper oxide, and manganese dioxide. Iron oxide, obtained from iron filings, produced a range of browns. From the copper came a brilliant green best seen when applied over a body previously covered with white slip or *engobe*. This effect is most noticeable in the late-nineteenth-century wares from the Shenandoah Valley of Virginia. The addition of manganese resulted in a brown to lustrous jet-black surface. Salve and preserve jars, as well as teapots made in Massachusetts, New Jersey, and Pennsylvania, were frequently treated in this manner. Manganese was also commonly used to daub the clear-glazed redware of Connecticut and Pennsylvania.

Colored glazes might be utilized to uniformly cover a piece of redware (as in the manganese teapots mentioned above); but, more often, they were mixed at random on the surface with a sponge or brush, a technique mimicking English Whieldon or tortoiseshell ware, just as the manganese finish reflected the influence of the all-black English Jackfield pottery.

Color might be employed in yet another way. A white slip made from *kaolin* or pipe clay was used either as a decorative element trailed or brushed on the clay surface, or as an opaque background (engobe) for more elaborate decoration.

Brushed white-slip decoration is rare. Archaeological excavations indicate that it was widely employed in New England during the eighteenth century, and a small jug brushed with an abstract leaf pattern is thought to be the oldest surviving example from the Norton Pottery at Bennington, Vermont (c. 1793–98). Almost a century later, it was popular for a time among the potters of the Strasburg area of Virginia.

Slip-decorated redware pie plates excavated at the site of the Nathaniel Rochester Pottery, Ontario County, N.Y., c. 1818–32. The "scroddled" finish on these plates is extremely uncommon in American redware.

Redware cream pot with an opaque white glaze and cobalt blue decoration attributed to Lorenzo Johnson, Erie County, N.Y., c. 1850–60. The cream pot form is more common in stoneware.

Slip-script-decorated pie plate, Norwalk, Ct., c. 1830–70. Plates decorated in this manner are characteristic of the Norwalk factory.

Enough for Rich Folks" or "Pony Up the Cash." Name and slogan plates were made primarily in the Connecticut Valley and in Pennsylvania. They are, today, among the most sought after pieces of redware. There are also examples of representational slip decoration, flowers and birds for the most part, from New Jersey, Pennsylvania, and North Carolina.

SGRAFFITO WARE

The most elaborate decoration on American redware combined slip with incised decoration. Referred to by early collectors as *tulip ware*, due to the preponderance of that motif (though some of the most important pieces feature humans and animals), or *scratched ware*, from the primary decorative method, these pie plates, jars, flower-

However, the creamy white slip was more often used in another manner. From the eighteenth century well into the nineteenth century, redware potters trailed decorative slip patterns across the surface of unglazed plates, platters, and shallow pans. Then, after the glaze had hardened and had been beaten down into the soft clay, the entire piece was given a coat of clear lead glaze. Firing created a design of slightly yellowish hue, which stood out sharply against the red-brown background.

Northern decorators utilized small baked-clay cups with one to a dozen holes fitted with turkey quills through which the slip flowed. By covering and uncovering these holes, the potter might vary the pattern he was creating. Southern potters, on the other hand, often used a cow horn cut open at the end.

While most slip-trailed decoration consisted primarily, if not exclusively, of abstract lines, some potters produced pieces embellished with names like "Lafayette," "City of Troy," and "Nancy," or slogans such as "This Is Good

Sgraffito- and slip-decorated redware pie plate, possibly by John Monday of Bucks County, Pa., c. 1820–30. Both the birds and the pot of flowers seen here are motifs frequently found on Pennsylvania sgraffito wares.

pots, and bowls were covered with a thick white engobe. After this opaque surface had air-dried, designs were scratched through it, revealing the contrasting redware body. The entire composition was then highlighted with slip or brush decoration in green, yellow, brown, or black. Following another drying period, the piece was given an overall clear lead glaze and fired.

Decoration could be as simple as a single flower, or complex—several horsemen, a colonial soldier and his lady. Typically, it was done freehand, but some artisans traced their basic sgraffito motif from a paper pattern, the outlines of which were punched into the clay with a pin or sharp stick (a technique also employed by some scrimshaw makers).

Sgraffito ware, particularly the more numerous plates, was intended for gifts and display, not use. Dates, the names of potters and/or owners, and a variety of homely slogans appear. Since most of the pieces were made by craftsmen of Germanic background, who were applying techniques utilized for centuries in Central Europe, the slogans are typically in German. Some reveal a surprisingly earthy sense of humor. For example:

He who would have something secret
Dare not tell it to his wife

I am a bird, of course
Whose bread I eat, his song I sing

Luck and misfortune
Are every morning our breakfast

(Edwin Atlee Barber, *Tulip Ware of the Pennsylvania-German Potters* [New York: Dover Publications, 1970].)

Since many dated examples from the eighteenth century exist, sgraffito ware as a body represents the earliest documented American redware. It is also the most expensive, with finer examples, rarely on the market, costing upwards of $30,000. While a few pieces from New Jersey and the Moravian shops of North Carolina are known, the vast majority of such work may be traced to the potters of eastern Pennsylvania.

FIRING

After decoration and glazing, green ware was returned to the drying shelves for a few more days. Then it was arranged in the oven or kiln for firing. The potter's kiln was the touchstone of his art. If the process of baking proved unsuccessful, as it frequently did through lack of skill or proper materials, all the work that had gone before was wasted. Consequently, considerable thought was given to the most efficient kiln design.

The earliest kiln, and the one which was used in the South and Southwest long after it had disappeared from New England, was the so-called groundhog kiln. This was a low rectangular brick or stone structure with an arched roof and a chimney at one end. At the other was an opening through which the green pottery could be inserted. The ware was stacked and thoroughly surrounded by dry wood. This tinder was then ignited and the entrance, except for a few ventilation holes, was sealed. As the fire burned, air circulation within the kiln caused the heat and flames to pass across the ware and out the chimney hole.

Uneven burning was always a problem with these cross-draft kilns, even when a firebox at the entrance end of the oven was substituted for the random distribution of fuel. Ware in one area would be overfired, while pieces somewhere else would not receive enough heat to mature properly.

Consequently, American potters, at an early date, began to employ updraft kilns, such as the one from the 1820s excavated near Rochester, New York. Round or oblong in shape, these were generally built on two levels, the lower

The sub-floor of the c. 1818–32 Nathaniel Rochester redware kiln in Ontario County, N.Y., during excavation by a team from the Rochester Museum and Science Center in 1973. Over the years the pottery site had become a forest.

Detail of the flues and fire-boxes at the Nathaniel Rochester kiln, an updraft design either beehive or bottle-shaped.

one of which contained one or more fireboxes constructed to feed the heat evenly into an upper "firing chamber" in which the ware was stacked.

Stacking, setting, or charging the kiln (several terms were employed for the procedure) prior to firing was an art in itself. Hundreds of articles varying greatly in shape and size had to be squeezed into a small area in such a way that they would not touch, to prevent glazed surfaces from adhering during firing.

Pieces were generally placed atop one another and separated by flat slabs of unglazed previously baked clay called *setting tiles*. Circular disks were employed to divide large jars, and three pointed *cockspurs* protected plates. Their char-

acteristic mark, three equally spaced dots, often appears on the bases of redware pie plates and bowls.

When all the ware had been placed in the kiln, the wood-burning fireboxes were ignited and the baking began. The fire had to be built up gradually over a considerable period in order to avoid the always present danger that too much heat too soon would cause the ware to collapse. Fires were maintained for eighteen to twenty-four hours, reaching a temperature of 1000–1,100°C. in the later stages. At this point the bricks of the kiln might turn white-hot, only the iron bands that bound them preventing their collapse. Throughout this period the potter and his assistants stood by, feeding the flames and

Lead-glazed redware jug, northeastern United States, c. 1820–40, marked D.A. BROWN *(possibly an owner). A classic example of kiln damage probably caused by an overheated kiln that "blistered" the ware.*

A large redware pot made and marked c. 1825–55 by Alvin Wilcox of West Bloomfield, New York. Note how the vessel has partially collapsed during firing. Such accidents were frequent, and damaged pieces were either thrown away or sold as "seconds."

checking the progress of the firing by means of test pieces that were attached to long wires so they could be withdrawn from the kiln.

It was hot, dirty work but not without its rewards. Particularly during the colder seasons, the kiln house became an oasis of warmth within which the potter, his family, friends, and neighbors ate, drank, sang, and danced while awaiting the conclusion of the firing.

At an appropriate time the fires were damped and the cooling period began. This usually took several days, at the end of which the kiln entrance was unblocked and the finished products were removed. If all had gone well, the unglazed pieces such as flowerpots would be a matt pinkish buff to red-brown in color (in general the higher the firing temperature the lighter the ware color). The hues of clear-lead-glazed objects would be enhanced by a brilliant glasslike surface, and colored glazes would gleam like jewels.

Certain special-order pieces would already have been spoken for. The rest of the kiln load would either be sold at the pottery or loaded upon horse-drawn wagons or riverboats to be peddled in the outlying neighborhood. Due to its fragile nature, redware was usually not sold far from its production source.

2

PRODUCTS OF THE REDWARE POTTERIES

FASCINATED BY GLAZES, slip writing, and sgrafitto, few collectors and dealers have any concept of, or appreciation for, the vast and varied output of the redware craft. An examination of almost any major private collection would leave one with the impression that potters made nothing but plates, platters, bowls, jars, crocks, and a few other items, all of which were highly decorated.

The truth is very different. During the eighteenth and nineteenth centuries the redware manufacturer often provided his community with the bulk of its domestic needs from tableware and storage vessels to writing and lighting equipment, sick-room necessities, dairying apparatus, musical instruments, toys, and even coffins! Most of these items were undecorated, and many were left unglazed as well.

The reasons for this vast and varied output lie in the nature of the craft and in the economics of the day. Clay is a highly flexible substance capable of taking many forms. Moreover, neither it nor the tools, glazes, and kilns used by the artisans were very expensive when compared with the capital necessary to establish and operate a glass factory, tinware shop, or iron foundry. Moreover, these latter were usually located at some considerable distance from rural and frontier communities.

Living directly among his potential customers, the potter could offer many items that were either unavailable at the time and place or were substantially more costly when made in other materials. Admittedly, however, the ceramic article was often less suitable to the task at hand, heavier or more fragile than its counterpart in glass, tin, or iron; and when the other materials did become available, pottery quickly lost favor among consumers. A case in point would be preserve jars for the storage of fruits

A group of unglazed redware miniatures, New England, c. 1880–1910. The jug in front is stenciled "Post Office Fair 1892." Pieces like this were sold or given away as souvenirs. The jug impressed "Boston Baked Beans" is an advertising item.

Flowerpot with attached saucer, Pennsylvania or Virginia, c. 1840–80. This piece is splashed with brown-and-white glaze; much of the white has pooled in this saucer.

and vegetables. Once made of clay in vast and varied numbers, these vanished from the scene following the introduction of the cheaper, lighter weight, and, most important, more sanitary airtight glass mason jar.

By 1900, the few remaining redware manufacturers were concentrating on flowerpots, decorative terra-cotta for use by builders, and small novelty items such as the miniature bean pots marked "Boston Baked Beans" that were made to be given away for promotional purposes.

However, the following should provide some idea of the central role that the eighteenth- and nineteenth-century redware potters played in providing for their neighbors' everyday needs. They might also offer thoughtful collectors an avenue toward broadening their holdings to more accurately reflect the true nature of the redware potter's craft.

TABLE WARES

Until replaced in the mid-nineteenth century, first by European imports and later by American-made ironstone china, redware dishes were the standard in every community. Pewter was expensive and hard to obtain. Wood or treen was readily available but difficult to keep clean. A potter who could turn out plates, cups, and bowls soon found employment. The Vermont-trained artisan Norman L. Judd, who in 1814 established himself in Rome, New York, then a rough boomtown on the road to the Western Reserve, reflected this demand in a letter to a friend:

We make Earthen Ware fast—have burned 8 kilns since the 8th of last May—amtg to $1500—Ware here is ready cash. It is now 8 o'clock at night, I have just done turning bowls—I rest across my mould bench while writing—no wonder if I do make wild shots . . . (Diary of Hiram Harwood, quoted in John Spargo, *The Potters and Potteries of Bennington* [New York: Dover Publications, 1972].)

Bowls

Bowls were made in many sizes for use in preparing, serving, and eating soup, stew, porridge, and other similar foods. Most were clear-glazed, usually both inside and out; though elaborately slip-decorated pieces were produced in Pennsylvania and Virginia and at the Moravian settlements in North Carolina. Smaller examples resembled Chinese "rice bowls" (like the black-glazed examples excavated at the site of the eighteenth-century Bayley Pottery in Newburyport, Massachusetts), while larger ones had wide rims and were relatively shallow, not unlike a modern soup bowl. Both forms are uncommon today.

The potter Elija Cornell of Ithaca, New York (father of Ezra, founder of Cornell University),

Redware mixing or serving bowl with mottled lead glaze, New England, c. 1830–60. Though common enough in yellow ware, these pieces are hard to find in red earthenware.

recorded in 1841 that small and pint bowls were among the items fired in his first kiln of that year; while as late as 1888 the firm of E. & C. Silknitter of Honeybrook, Pennsylvania, was selling pint bowls at fifty cents per dozen, or a nickel each.

Plates

Also called dishes, these were another staple of the nineteenth-century craftsman. As late as the 1850s, the Huntington, New York, pottery, then managed by Frederick Caire, was offering plates in diameters ranging from eight to fourteen inches. The larger size sold for $1.50 per dozen. Most plates were clear-glazed, though, again, examples from Pennsylvania and North Carolina were often finely slip-decorated. Eating plates can be distinguished from pie plates by their shallowness and wider rims.

Porringers

Generally considered the forerunner of the cup, the porringer is a squat bowl-shaped vessel with a flat, triangular tablike handle. It was used for eating porridge, soup, and gruel. The form is based on earlier silver and pewter examples. A clear-glazed porringer incised "A G/1720" was excavated from the site of the Yorktown, Virginia, pottery. It is believed to be the oldest dated example of American redware.

This is a unique example, and later so-called porringers have ear handles similar to those on modern teacups, though they retain the squat, bowl-like body.

Cups

By the early 1800s, American potters were making cups not unlike those used today, though generally with thicker, shallower bodies. In 1837, the Athens, New York, firm of Clark &

Fox offered these in pint and half-pint sizes. Matching saucers were not advertised and do not appear to have been commonly available, though they are known to have been made by the Moravians. Cups were glazed inside and out, some in clear lead, others in several colors to create a marbleized effect.

Mugs

Mugs, either cylindrical in form or slightly ovoid, were produced in great quantity for use in the home and in public houses and taverns. Ranging in capacity from a half-pint to a quart, they might be clear- or black-glazed, manganese-splotched or sponged in green and brown on a white engobe, as at Bethabara in North Carolina. John Bell of Waynesboro, Pennsylvania, even applied sprigged figures, eagles, and human heads to his mugs; while other Pennsylvania craftsmen incised designs and appropriate slogans on those intended as gifts.

Mugs were subjected to hard use, and only a fraction of the many thousands made can be found today. Among the rare marked examples are ones from the Bell family kilns in Virginia and Pennsylvania.

Beakers and Goblets

Though never as satisfactory as glass, cone-shaped redware beakers or tumblers and footed goblets were used at some country tables. Most were undecorated, like the lead-glazed example that bears the stamp of the Wilcox Pottery of West Bloomfield, New York. There are, however, scratch-decorated pieces from Pennsylvania, and Moravian tumblers from North Carolina are sponged in green and brown. These

Lead-glazed redware mug, New York or New Jersey, c. 1830–60. Mugs were produced in great quantity by every pottery, yet today few survive, probably due to rough handling in taverns and public houses.

Slip-decorated platter and pie plates, Norwalk, Ct., c. 1830–80. The wavy pattern is sometimes referred to by collectors as "ocean waves."

Platters

Round platters slipped in red, black, and brown over white were the only decorated wares found at the eighteenth-century Yorktown pottery site; and oval, oblong, or octagonal platters were made well into the nineteenth century. Those most sought after are the slip-script examples from Connecticut and New Jersey, some of which bear a humorous message such as "Hard Times in Jersey." Sizes range from twelve to

latter tumblers were valued at "four pence each" in an 1801 inventory. The Moravians even produced some dainty footed wineglasses. All such pieces are extremely rare.

twenty-two inches. Platters called *flat pans* were being sold by the Norwalk, Connecticut, pottery in 1864 at $1.20 to $6.40 per dozen, depending upon size.

Serving Dishes

Other than platters, there was a wide variety of vessels used to serve hot and cold foods. Many were simply bowls with or without handles that were often glazed only on the interior. Examples dating to the eighteenth century were excavated at both Yorktown, Virginia, and Bethabara, North Carolina. At a later date, deep fully glazed oval serving and baking dishes, more often found in ironstone or yellow ware, were also made from the red-burning clay. Some of these dishes were divided so that two vegetables might be served at the same time. Bread came to the table in a pierced or openwork basket with flaring rim, while handled openwork compotes were used for fruit and large dome-covered tureens were used for stew or casserole dishes. Perhaps least common were lead-glazed pedestal-base cake stands.

Trivets

Trivets or hot plates, like so many other unusual redware forms, seem to have been confined in their production to Virginia and Pennsylvania. Unglazed disk-shaped examples appear often in shops and at shows. Glazed trivets are much less common, though one in brown and yellow bears the stamp of John Bell, Waynesboro, Pennsylvania.

Egg Cups

Redware egg cups, which look much like the modern version, were a late addition to the potter's repertory. Pennsylvania examples were generally clear-glazed; but one in cream, brown, and green is attributed to the pottery of Samuel Bell and Sons, Strasburg, Virgina, c. 1882–1908.

Teapots and Coffeepots

Though difficult to manufacture, teapots and coffeepots were in sufficient demand to justify the effort. Teapots are found in greatest quantity. Some, like the Whately, Massachusetts, products, were thrown on the wheel with straight or onion-form sides with an applied tubular spout. However, many potters such as John Mann of Rahway, New Jersey, employed molds to cast more elaborate examples. Most teapots were covered with an overall black glaze, though clear- and color-glazed examples will be found. Teapots appear in the inventory of the Moravian Pottery at Bethabara, North Carolina, as early as 1789, and in 1864 the Smith Pottery at Norwalk, Connecticut, was selling them in two sizes at $1.75 and $2.25 per dozen.

Coffeepots were usually turned and were much less common. Several finely shaped and glazed examples are in Pennsylvania museums, and the potter John Vickers of Chester County offered them for sale in an 1835 advertisement at $3.50 per dozen or $.38 each, making them the most expensive items he sold.

Sugar Bowls

Perhaps the most elaborate serving piece to grace the colonial table was the sugar bowl. Sugar was for many years a costly luxury, and those who had it flaunted it. North Carolina Moravian potters made onion-shaped bowls with horizontal loop handles, dome tops, and floral and geometric decoration in green, white, and brown. Pennsylvania examples were more elaborate with double-walled piercework-decorated sides, sgraffito and slip decoration, dome tops often terminating in openwork or animal figures, and slogans such a "A souvenir of the year 1857," which reflected that many such pieces were expensive gifts. However, not all sugar bowls were so elaborate. Enos Smedley of Chester County, Pennsylvania, sold plain ones at only sixty cents per dozen in 1834.

Salts

Another prized commodity in the early years of settlement was salt. Typically, a table would be set with a large master salt. This would be wide and squat without a foot, no doubt to minimize spilling. Smaller individual salts, either of similar shape or looking like small bowls mounted on a turned pedestal foot (such as those made in the second half of the nineteenth century by Carl Mehwaldt of Bergholz, New York) would be filled from this and set at each place. The Beth-abara, North Carolina, kiln advertised such "standing salts" in 1803; and John Vickers of Chester County, Pennsylvania, sold them for just nineteen cents per dozen in 1835. At a later date there were also casters or salt shakers similar in form to modern ones. None of these forms are readily found today.

Pitchers

Every redware potter made pitchers in sizes ranging from tiny half-pint creamers to great two-gallon cider containers. Most small and larger ones were hand-thrown, although the popular quart-size pitchers were frequently cast in molds that left embossed floral or pictorial designs on the vessel's surface. Described as "Fancy Pitchers" in a mid-nineteenth-century Huntington, New York, pottery price list, these were given a clear or brown glaze and sold for $2.50 per dozen, while their turned counterparts cost a dollar less.

Most pitchers, like those made in the 1870s by the St. Charles, Missouri, potter, Joseph Oser, were dipped in a clear lead glaze. For something "fancy" one turns again to Pennsylvania where colored slip and, at times, sgraffito decoration were common. Nineteenth-century pitchers attributed to the Salem, North Carolina, potter Rudolph Christ were also elaborately decorated with floral motifs, geometric devices, and wavy lines in white applied via the slip cup to a darker clay body.

Most spectacular of pitchers are the so-called puzzle jugs, which were regarded as a tour de force by Pennsylvania potters. Holes in the neck of each piece made it appear impossible to pour without flooding one's neighbors; but, in fact, interior tubing directed the liquid (usually beer or hard cider) around the perforations and safely into the glass or mug. In keeping with the effort it took to design such a system, the pitchers were richly glazed and often sgraffito-decorated as well. An example by the Bucks County potter, Philip Kline, now in the Philadelphia Museum of Art collection, bears an incised eagle and the logo "Liberty/ P × K May the 5 1809," while on the base may be found the potter's mark— PHILIP KLINE HIS MUGE.

Covered, manganese-splotched red-ware sugar bowl, Berks County, Pa., c. 1840–70. Sugar bowls were among the most interesting pieces made by Pennsylvania potters.

Redware pitchers. Left, *Missouri, c. 1870–85;* center and right, *northeastern, c. 1850–80. The two smaller examples are mugs onto which the potter has pulled a pouring spout.*

A related form, the beer pitcher, had a covered spout and sometimes a lid to prevent the beer from going flat. The Hart Pottery at Sherburne, New York, made these in Albany slip–glazed redware during the 1870s and 1880s. Other than for flowerpots and stove tubes, these were the only redware items made at this stoneware manufactory.

COOKING AND BAKING UTENSILS

Though less durable than stoneware or cast iron, redware found a place in the kitchen, particularly in baking where such vessels retained an even heat thought to facilitate the preparation of cakes and pies. Nevertheless, the introduction of glass and tin gradually limited the potter's market, though the ubiquitous bean pot remained popular well into the twentieth century.

Bean Pots

Baked beans have been a staple in the United States for generations, and the redware bean pot is a commonly found item. Lead-glazed inside and out or only on the interior, with one, two, or no handles, these squat, rounded vessels ranged in capacity from a pint to a gallon and came with matching tops. Also appropriately known as "bean bakers," they were being offered in the 1880s by the Monmouth, Maine, potter, George L. Safford at $1.75 per dozen. Pennsylvania examples are sometimes manganese-splotched, but decoration is rare in these purely utilitarian pieces. An interesting and frequently seen variation is the miniature version, usually about two inches high. Used to promote the sale of baked beans or as souvenirs sold at local sites, these are, along with chamber pots, the most common American ceramic miniatures.

Unglazed redware single-handled bean pot of a form made from Maine to Missouri, c. 1680–1920. These pieces are rarely marked and almost impossible to attribute.

Lead-glazed, double-handled bean pot, New York or New Jersey, c. 1840–70. Most bean pots had one or no handles.

Stew Pots

A related though usually somewhat larger form was the stew pot that was used to cook meat and vegetables. This was a tall ovoid vessel, often with small horizontal handles that fit closely against the neck. Sizes ranged from a quart to a gallon and a half, and there were matching tops. A marked example by the Maine potter John M. Safford is impressed "Stew Pot No. 3," lest one mistake its purpose. Moreover, this example departs from the usual conservative decorative style found among Maine craftsmen in that it is glazed in pale green and decorated with bands of punchwork rosettes.

Pipkins

An early form still in use today is the pipkin. This oddly named vessel is a squat, covered cooking pot with a hollow handle to allow for the escape of steam. Found in several sizes, most often one pint to one gallon, pipkins were customarily clear-glazed inside and out. In 1888, the Silknitter Pottery at Honeybrook, Pennsylvania, sold the gallon size for $2.25 per dozen.

Pudding Pans

Another form frequently encountered today is the pudding pan. These squat, cylindrical vessels with outwardly tapering sides are more pots than pans. They were used primarily in making Indian pudding, a thick mixture of milk, corn, and butter. Some examples are glazed only on the inside, but most are fully finished; and New England examples often are manganese-splotched. Their cost seems to have varied widely, for the Norwalk, Connecticut, pottery sold them in the late 1860s for ninety cents to two dollars per dozen, while the Brosius kiln at Kennett Square, Pennsylvania, was offering them a decade later for forty-eight to ninety-two cents a dozen.

Bakers

Square or oval baking dishes (which might also double as serving utensils) were often referred to as "bakers." Ranging in size from eight to fourteen inches, they were a product of the second half of the nineteenth century and are more often seen in ironstone or yellow ware. All were clear-glazed.

Nappys

Cooking was also done in nappys, round deep dishes with tapering sides set at about a 25° angle. They were frequently found in nests of six to eight varying sizes, more typically in yellow earthenware; though the Huntington, New York, pottery listed them in the 1860s as available in two sizes at $.87 and $1.25 a dozen. Nappys were fully glazed in lead, sometimes with black-daubed decoration.

Roasting Pans and Skillets

Large oblong roasting pans without covers and with a lift handle at one end and a drainway for fat at the other were occasionally made in North Carolina and Pennsylvania, as were skillets—shallow pans mounted on three feet and with a hollow pipkinlike handle. Both forms were characteristically glazed inside only, and both are rare today.

Pie Plates

From the collector's point of view the single most important redware form is the pie plate. Fruit and meat pies were a staple of the European diet long before this country was settled, and the perception of the pie plate as a tour de force of the potter's art suitable for gift giving was well established both in England and in Central Europe.

English potters brought the tradition of the

Clear-glazed redware pipkin with matching cover; Pennsylvania or Ohio, c. 1860–80. These cooking vessels are uncommon.

Cooking and table ware: left, a manganese-splotched pudding pan; center rear, a large nappy 12 inches in diameter; and right, a "rice bowl" form eating bowl.

Slip-script-decorated pie plate, Norwalk, Ct., c. 1830–70. Spelling was not a strong point with many early potters!

slip-script pie plate to New England, where it reached its fullest development in the Connecticut Valley area. Names and slogans in white slip on the red-clay ground might commemorate a community ("New York City," "City of Troy"); an important historical figure ("Lafay-

ette"); favorite foods ("Mince Pie," "Clams & Oysters"); call for political change ("Cheap Money") or, most often, simply bear the name of a recipient ("Mary's Dish").

Potters working in the English manner carried this tradition throughout New England and into New York and New Jersey; however, the most spectacular pie plates of all were made in Pennsylvania. Slip- and sgraffito-decorated examples from this area were so well thought of that the Philadelphia potter Jonathan Durell advertised, upon his arrival in Manhattan in 1773, that he could provide ware ". . . equal to the best imported from Philadelphia. . . ."

From the 1770s until the 1830s, Pennsylvania craftsmen turned out thousands of these elaborate pie plates, most of which were "for pretty,"

Slip-script-decorated pie plate, Pennsylvania, probably Philadelphia, c. 1830–40. The Wildey family was prominent at this time in Philadelphia politics.

designed to flatter a mantel or cupboard rather than a hot and sooty oven. Many were signed by such renowned artisans as Georg Hubener, David Spinner, John Nase, and John Leidy, and bore traditional epithets like "I cook what I can/ If my sow will not eat, my husband will" and "If loving were unwholesome/ Surely the doctor would avoid it." Some even expressed the craftsman's feelings about his trade and customers, such as "This pot is made of earth/ And when it breaks the potter laughs."

Slip-decorated pie plates of high quality were also produced in the Shenandoah Valley of Virginia and in North Carolina. But the majority made everywhere were the utilitarian-type lead-glazed only on the interior and with coggled or pinched rims. These, including miniatures, range in diameter from three to twelve inches.

Most collectors are precluded from owning sgraffito-decorated pie plates by their rarity and by prices ranging into five figures. Even the slip-script examples are bringing prices in the low thousands. However, undecorated plates are still modestly priced.

Cake and Jelly Molds

Cake molds or bundt pans are among the most common types of redware. They are usually circular, with a central column frequently spiral-shaped, hence the name *Turk's cap mold* often applied to this type. Used primarily for sponge cake, such pieces were often slip-cast (a plaster mold used at the Perine Pottery in Baltimore is owned by the Maryland Historical Society) and given a clear or manganese-splotched finish. However, some in multicolored glazes will be found. A few marked examples, by John Bell and Alvin Wilcox, for example, are known. Described as "moulded cake dishes" in an 1837 price list, these were sold in three sizes by the Athens, New York, firm of Clark & Fox. Examples available today range in diameter from four to fourteen inches.

Similar but smaller round lead-glazed molds with patterned interiors were used in the preparation of jellies. These were also made in yellow ware and ironstone; and almost identical ones in tin, aluminum, or glass are in use today. Also,

A group of three sponge cake or food molds, northeast, c. 1840–80. Often termed Turk's cap molds, *these are found in great variety of color and form.*

small handleless cups covered with a clear glaze, either on the interior or inside and out, were used to prepare custard. These, too, closely resemble contemporary examples.

Less often seen are figural molds. These may take the shape of a fish, an ear of corn, or even a turkey. They were employed primarily in the making of pudding and are seldom, if ever, marked. A related form is the muffin pan, which was glazed only on the interior and looked like a flattened cluster of grapes.

Rarest of all are redware butter prints used to stamp the shape of a flower, leaf, bird, or animal on a block of fresh butter and oblong springerle molds that could impress a design in the top of a cake or large cookie. Both forms were traditionally carved from wood, and the more fragile ceramic examples seem never to have found favor with customers. However, prints in the form of a six-pointed star were made by John Bell of Waynesboro, Pennsylvania.

MISCELLANEOUS KITCHEN ITEMS

The potter made other things for the housewife, some of which we would hardly expect to find in redware. There were, for example, grease skimmers resembling flat, perforated plates with tab handles. They must have been both awkward and fragile, for few survived. The useful funnel also has a long history in the medium. Sherds from one were dug up at the Yorktown, Virginia, pottery (c. 1720–45), and another was found (in pieces) at the late-eighteenth-century Bethabara, North Carolina, site. Most were clear-glazed, but examples daubed in manganese on a green ground from Pennsylvania are known.

Colanders, though rather uncommon today in redware, were made in great quantity. They were found at Yorktown, and were still being made by various late-nineteenth-century kilns.

The form, however, varied substantially. Examples made and marked by the potter Moulton Bodge of Fayette, Maine, were simply perforated milk pans, as were most made at Galena, Illinois. Late-nineteenth-century ones tended to resemble mixing bowls, while in New Jersey and Pennsylvania the shape might be that of a large chamber pot, sometimes mounted on peg-like feet. Whatever the form, colanders were typically given a monochromatic glaze. Batter jugs, though much more common in stoneware, were also seen in the softer medium; and the bullet-shaped molds in which raw sugar cones were formed for the colonial kitchen were also sometimes made of redware and left unglazed. They are very rare today.

DAIRYING VESSELS

Prior to the advent of the commercial dairy in the late nineteenth century, most rural families kept cows and sometimes goats from which they obtained a variety of food products. Such redware items as milk pans, cream and butter cups, churns and strainers, facilitated this process.

Milk Pans

Shallow redware vessels with sloping sides two to four inches high were used in separating milk from cream. Fresh milk would be poured into these basinlike vessels, and the heavy cream could be skimmed off as it rose to the top. Eighteenth- and early-nineteenth-century milk pans were hand-thrown, glazed only on the inside, and quite large—often as much as eighteen inches in diameter. An example made at the Sampson Pottery in Hartford, Maine, now at the Maine State Museum, is nearly seventeen inches across and dates c. 1830–40.

By mid-century, smaller and lighter pans with higher sides were sold in nests of four or five. These were often drape- or slip-molded.

The Mormon potter Frederick F. Hansen was turning them out at Brigham City, Utah, in the 1860s, and in the 1870s Edwin Brosius of Kennett Square, Pennsylvania, made milk pans in five sizes from ten to fourteen inches in diameter. Even the largest sold for only $2.40 per dozen, or $.25 each. By this time, though, tin pans, which were both lighter and easier to clean, were replacing the ceramic ones.

Cream and Butter Pots

Milk and cream were placed in tall, slightly ovoid pots, which were unglazed on the exterior and had rounded rims (so that cloth or wax paper might be tied about them to keep out dirt or insects), and then stored until used in spring houses or cool cellars. Often referred to simply as "pots" or "high pots," these vessels ranged in capacity up to three gallons. They were also used to preserve other commodities.

Fresh sweet butter was stored in cylindrical pots with closely fitting lids. These butter pots or "coolers" were made by nearly every redware manufacturer. The pottery at Huntington, New York, offered them in the 1860s in three sizes—one, one and a half, and two gallons—just as the Athens, New York, pottery had in 1837. Most were clear-glazed, though some may be found with manganese splotching.

Churns

Though they continued to be made until the late nineteenth century by some southern potters, redware churns were never very practical. They were simply too fragile to take the pounding necessary to turn cream or milk into butter. Customers preferred stoneware or wooden ones. Remaining examples range from ten to twenty-four inches in height and are lead-glazed, some with manganese daubing. I know of one marked example, by the potter Lorenzo Johnson of Erie County, New York.

Cheese Strainers

Rarely seen today, cheese strainers were shallow perforated vessels, usually with a single handle. They looked most like a squat colander and were used in draining the whey from fresh cheese. They were finished with a clear lead glaze. Tin cheese strainers replaced them at a relatively early date.

STORAGE VESSELS

Probably the oldest and certainly the most common of redware are the various jugs, jars, pots,

Small butter churn, possibly New York or Vermont, c. 1840–65. Due to their fragile nature relative to the task performed, few redware churns have survived.

and crocks used for storing food, drink, and other items. Until the introduction of electricity, food preservation depended primarily upon ice, available mostly in northern climes, salting, drying, and storage (after cooking at a high temperature) in airtight containers.

Though the potter did his best to answer these needs, the rapid disappearance of ceramic storage vessels after the invention of the glass mason jar, the airtight tin can, and the electric refrigerator indicates his limitations.

Jugs

Jugs, used for the storage of everything from water to wine, whiskey, milk, vinegar, oil, and even roofing or caulking tar are among the earliest of American redware. A late-seventeenth-century example has been excavated in Manhattan, jug fragments were recovered at the site of the Bayley Pottery (c. 1723–99) in Newburyport, Massachusetts, and Andrew Duche reportedly made a similar item at Savannah, Georgia, before 1738.

Redware jugs range in size from a half-pint to one gallon; larger examples are rare due both to their weight and fragile nature. The earliest are ovoid or egg-shaped in form, assuming a ball shape in the early 1800s. By 1840, most had only the suggestion of taper (though there are exceptions, such as the lovely ovoid jugs thrown by John Hammett at Belmont, Wisconsin, in the 1850s), and those few produced after 1860 were usually straight-sided like their stoneware counterparts.

Though the majority were given a clear lead or black manganese glaze, some jugs, particularly from New England, were elaborately splashed with green, yellow, brown, and black.

As one might expect with vessels made in so many different places, prices varied greatly. When the potter Reuben Thorpe of Turner, Maine, died in 1823, sixteen of his two-quart jugs were valued at only seventy-five cents. On the other hand, Frederick Caire of Huntington, New York, sold the same size at two dollars per dozen in the 1860s.

Variations on the form include molasses jugs

A group of manganese-glazed storage vessels, New England or Pennsylvania, c. 1830–70. From left to right: a straight-sided preserve jar, a semi-ovoid jug, and an ovoid preserve jar or vase.

Lead-glazed redware preserve jar with touches of cream and green in the manner of Chinese Celedon ware, New York, c. 1830–60. ▶

with a lipped spout to facilitate pouring; and harvest jugs, with a strap handle running side to side across the top of the piece rather than the customary ear-shaped handle, and two opposing spouts, the larger one for filling. There is also the so-called field jug that has two handles rather than one. The addition of a lower spigot hole makes this a type of watercooler.

Preserve Jars

Jars may generally be distinguished from pots and crocks by their smaller openings or mouths. Many different jar types have been used in food preservation. Most earlier examples were somewhat ovoid, but eighteenth-century straight-sided jars are known; in fact graduated sets of black-glazed ones are among the more interesting of this type. These were rarely marked, though Darlington Cope of Chester County, Pennsylvania, impressed his name on the base of his jars. Whatever its body form, the jar will have a pronounced lip (to facilitate sealing it with a piece of cloth or oiled paper). Some examples will have turned inner ledges on which matching lids rested, while late-nineteenth-century "wax sealers" have double rims around and over which a tin disk was sealed with wax to create an airtight bond.

Large jars of several gallon capacity with free-standing handles were used for storage of oils, as well as dry materials like grain and even coffee. One found at Bethabara, North Carolina, had the following inscription:

Today we celebrate Lovefeast.
That you can tell by the good turnout.
When this urn is full of coffee
How few here will be missed.
And when it's full, then I'm right there.
And when it's empty, then we'll sing Hallelujah.
March 12, 1821.
(John Bivins, Jr., *The Moravian Potters of North Carolina* [Chapel Hill: The University of North Carolina Press, 1972].)

These larger vessels were usually glazed only on the inside. On the other hand, nearly all jars of a gallon capacity or less were fully finished. This decoration might be simple manganese splotching or quite elaborate as with some sgraffito-decorated Pennsylvania examples and the richly splashed orange, green, and yellow pieces made in the various kilns at Galena, Illinois.

Most shops made jars of pint, quart, two-quart, and gallon capacity. In the 1880s George Safford of Monmouth, Maine, sold the gallon size for $2.00 per dozen, while the same size but with the addition of a matching lid brought $2.70 in 1864 at the Norwalk, Connecticut, factory.

Pots

Open mouthed semiovoid pots with thick everted rims served many useful purposes. Bean and stew pots for cooking and cream and butter pots used in dairying have been discussed earlier. Other pots varying in size from one-quarter to four-gallon capacity were used for storage of both soft foods and such things as rice, oats, and barley. These were seldom provided with matching lids and often were given only an interior glaze.

Pots were by far the most frequently made objects at the Moravian settlement of Wachovia in North Carolina. In 1789, the kiln house inventory there listed eight different sizes at prices of from 5 pence to 2 shillings apiece. By 1864 the Norwalk Pottery could boast of six sizes ranging in price from $.75 to $3.60 per dozen.

Crocks

Some think of the straight-sided storage crock as a later development of the more rounded pot. In fact, the two forms have existed together for hundreds of years. Lead-glazed examples of what we would term a crock were among the finds at the site of the eighteenth-century York-town, Virginia, pottery. The term *crock* seems to be what's new, having been developed during the mid-nineteenth century to refer to the familiar stoneware storage vessels.

Perhaps the distinction lies in the method of covering the mouth of the vessel. Stoneware crocks traditionally came with matching tops, where redware pots usually did not. The few late-nineteenth-century redware examples that mimic the stoneware form also have matching lids. Interestingly enough, I have yet to see a redware pottery price list that uses the term *crock*, and marked examples are rare, though I know of a few from the Morganville, New York, kiln.

Redware watercoolers and rundlets, c. 1830–50. Left to right: manganese-glazed rundlet, Pennsylvania; clear-lead-glazed watercooler, Ohio; elaborately turned rundlet in mustard glaze, Maine. These vessels were used to store water and alcoholic beverages, such as rum, whiskey, or wine.

Tubs

An unusual form in redware is the butter tub. This is a straight-sided crocklike form with opposing rope handles attached to the rim top. Marked, slip-decorated examples were made at the Solomon Bell pottery in Strasburg, Virginia. Relatively small (five by six inches), they were used in the temporary storage and serving of butter.

Watercoolers and Rundlets

The classic barrel-shaped watercooler used to store and serve water, rum, wine, or hard cider is rare in redware. I have seen few examples above a foot in height, though stoneware coolers may be twice that large. The explanation is probably again weight and fragility. A few lead-glazed gallon coolers may be found, but they are not common.

On the other hand, the roughly pint-sized rundlet or swigler, which is really a miniature cooler complete with barrel form and top and bottom bung holes, is fairly common. These

vessels were used to carry rum and other hard liquor. Most are in a black glaze, but examples exuberantly splashed in olive, green, red, and brown may be found. They were not production items and do not appear in potters' price lists.

A rare and interesting variation, more often seen in stoneware, is the water monkey or blind pig, a large rundlet resting on its side and mounted on four stubby feet.

Flasks and Bottles

In 1864, the Smith Pottery at Norwalk, Connecticut, was advertising pint and half-pint bottles at sixty and forty-five cents per dozen, respectively. As is so often the case, we cannot be sure to what this referred. Redware potters made two basic forms: flask and bottle. The former was a flattened ovoid much like a squashed handleless jug and generally similar to the hip

Two rare redware ring flasks, c. 1830–50: top, Georgia or North Carolina in an ash glaze; bottom, clear-lead-glazed from Massachusetts.

flasks produced throughout the nineteenth century by American glass houses. Flasks were generally clear- or black-glazed or splashed with manganese. While the majority (like the marked examples from John Safford, II, of Monmouth, Maine) were thrown, pressed or slip-cast examples with raised decoration were produced at, among other places, the Poughkeepsie pottery of John B. Caire.

The bottle form might resemble a glass sack bottle of the early 1800s or, at a later date, the very common stoneware ginger beer bottle. There were also short-necked, cylindrical ink and blacking bottles no more than three or four inches high. These utilitarian forms were seldom advertised, and generally were simply glazed in lead or manganese.

Rarest of all are ring bottles, circular vessels of doughnut shape, sometimes mounted on stubby feet. These were hooked onto the saddle pommel when traveling and were used to contain water or something harder, depending on the rigors of the journey. Usually clear-lead-glazed, the form was made in the Appalachians late into the nineteenth century.

BATH AND SICKROOM ITEMS

The redware potter attempted to provide for all his clients' needs, and these included a variety of bath and sickroom items, some of which collectors may regard as unappealing. However, the quantity in which several of these pieces may still be found indicates how important they once were.

Washbowls

Among the most desirable of all American redware are the spectacular pitcher and bowl sets manufactured in the Strasburg area of Virginia in the late nineteenth century. The bowls often had large strap handles for carrying and inset soap dishes, while the classic form pitchers bore complex handles. Both were typically splashed in green and brown on a cream ground. Best-known among the makers were the Bell family, though Jacob Eberly and Anthony Baecher made similar ware. Marked examples will be found.

Washbowls were also made by northern potters. In 1864, the Smith Pottery at Norwalk, Connecticut, advertised them in five sizes: pint, quart, three pint, half-gallon, and gallon. Most expensive were those of gallon capacity at $2.10 per dozen. All were lead-glazed.

Barber Bowls and Shaving Mugs

Made primarily in Pennsylvania, barber bowls were highly personal and highly decorated. They resembled a pie plate in form, except for the semicircular notch in one side for the patron's neck. Sgraffito and slip decoration was the rule; and slogans, such as "You poor beard, must leave my hide" on an eighteenth-century example by John Leidy I, were customary. Few examples will be found outside museum collections.

Shaving mugs were more widely manufactured. In form they resembled a common cylindrical mug with, however, a small soap pocket either within the mug or protruding from one side. Though Pennsylvania pieces might be richly glazed, most New England examples were given a clear-lead or black finish. In 1834, Enos Smedley of Chester County, Pennsylvania, listed the more common examples at $1.20 per dozen.

Soap Dishes

Round, oval, and oblong glazed soap dishes were made in imitation of more common examples in Rockingham Ware. Some were hand-thrown or hand-built, but most were cast in molds. The 1853 inventory of the estate of the potter Frederick Swope, of Lancaster County, Pennsylvania, contained several such pieces.

Washboards

Redware washboards were uncommon. These consisted of a square or oblong slab of clay, clear-glazed or splashed in manganese and mounted within the usual wooden washboard frame. Larger examples measure about eight by ten inches, while a smaller six-inch variety may have been intended for children. Most examples have been found in Ohio or Pennsylvania, and the presence of wire nails in the frame indicates they date to the late nineteenth century.

Spittoons

Spittoons or cuspidors were made in vast numbers, reflecting a society where most men and

Manganese-daubed redware child's washboard, Pennsylvania or Ohio, c. 1880–1900. The presence of wire nails indicates that these pieces date to the turn of the century.

Redware spittoon bearing the mark of the Morganville, New York, pottery, c. 1870–1900.

some women chewed tobacco. They were both hand-thrown and cast. The Gast Pottery at Lancaster, Pennsylvania, turned out richly glazed, molded examples from 1860 until the shop closed down in 1913. There were also women's sizes, three to five inches across, and, even less attractive, covered spit cups (looking just like a cup with a domed cover) for the many tuberculosis sufferers.

Chamber Pots and Bedpans

Handled chamber pots came in several sizes. Smaller versions should not be confused with porringers, as the pottys always have a wide, flaring rim. E. Stanley Grier of Chester County, Pennsylvania, offered these "chamber mugs" for $1.25 to $2.00 per dozen as late as 1905. Darlington Cope, also of Chester County, marked his black-glazed examples.

For the invalid, there were circular bedpans with hollow tubular handles. Bedpans were in sufficient demand to appear as production items in both the Athens, New York, pottery price list of 1837 and that published in 1864 by the Huntington, New York, factory. They were not inexpensive. Huntington offered two sizes at $3.60 and $4.50 per dozen. Interestingly enough, most chamber pots and bedpans seen today are richly splashed in manganese over a dark red clay. Despite this attractive glaze, few collectors are interested in the form.

Bedroom or sickroom utensils. Left to right: child's chamber pot, bedpan, and adult's chamber pot. All are from Connecticut or Pennsylvania, manganese-decorated and date c. 1840–90.

Invalid Cups

Another item for the use of the invalid or the very young was the invalid cup or pap boat. An example in a yellow glaze bears the mark of the Pennsylvania potter John Bell. It looks like a porringer cup with a curved tubular spout exiting from the lower body. A sick person could suck milk or gruel from this vessel.

Hot-Water Bottles

Hot-water bottles and foot warmers were oval or in the shape of a loaf of bread and had a spout for filling at the top. These essentially similar forms were usually clear- or black-glazed and are rare today.

LIGHTING DEVICES

A substantial number of lighting devices were produced by American potters; however, since these were rarely marked and usually resemble European forms of the same period, it is often difficult to sort out homegrown examples.

The potter Carl Mehwaldt of Bergholz, New York, made what is, perhaps, the rarest of our lighting devices: a chandelier. Designed for installation in a local church, it was four feet in diameter, hand-modeled, and held two rows of candles.

Mehwaldt was of German extraction, and most earthen lighting devices appear to have been made in areas where Germanic settlements were established.

Fat or Grease Lamps

The standard lamp form both in Central Europe and among these immigrants consisted of a shallow bowl with spout for a wick mounted on a saucerlike base. One or two loop handles facilitated handling. Animal fat or cooking oil was burned to provide a smokey light. Most examples were clear-glazed, though an unglazed redware piece from the Morgantown, West Virginia, pottery of John W. Thompson is in the Smithsonian collection. There were also ceramic stands on which sheet iron Betty lamps rested. These consisted of a round flat dishlike top and base joined by a turned column.

Candlesticks

Two redware candlestick types are known. The first is baluster form with a wide disklike base, while the second is shaped like a shallow cup with an inset candle socket and is related to the brass or tin chamber stick. Both are usually clear- or manganese-glazed, though splotch-decorated Pennsylvania specimens can be found.

Manganese-glazed baluster form candlestick, Pennsylvania or North Carolina, c. 1810–40. Candlesticks are exceedingly rare, and almost all are from these two states.

Despite the fact that such lighting devices were made as far back as the eighteenth century at the Moravian settlements in North Carolina, they were apparently not standard production items and do not appear in pottery price lists or inventories.

Fishing Lamps

A redware light used in night fishing or gigging (fish spearing), consisting of several spouts extending from a large round fount with strap handle, is at the Chester County Historical Society. It burned fat or oil-soaked rushes. The form is more often seen in sheet iron or brass.

Candlemolds

The tin or pewter mold in which wax candles were formed is a common sight. However, a few potters made redware molds. Glazed only on the interior, the individual mold tubes were mounted in groups of twenty-four or thirty-six in a wooden frame. Marked examples are known from Alvin Wilcox at West Bloomfield, New York; and ones marked SMEDLEY & CO. are thought to have originated with Enos Smedley of Chester County, Pennsylvania.

Match Holders

Glazed ceramic match holders were produced by a few potters in Pennsylvania and the South. Most were slab-formed and given a clear lead glaze. Rare examples, possibly designed as gifts, were more elaborate with multicolored glazes and hand-formed details.

FLOWERPOTS, VASES, AND URNS

By the last quarter of the nineteenth century, the few redware makers remaining in business had focused their attention on the flowerpots needed by farmers, florists, and householders. Wheel-thrown at first and then more often cast in molds, these pots (often with attached saucers) and associated urns, fern stands, and hanging flower baskets were primarily utilitarian, plain, and glazed only on the interior.

However, ornamental pots were made at an early date (a marked example from the 1830s by the potter Austin Hempstead of Greenport, Long Island, is in the collection of the Suffolk County, New York, Historical Society); and these are among the more interesting examples of decorated redware.

In the Shenandoah Valley of Virginia, the Bell family and their competitors, Anthony Baecher and the Eberly clan, turned out many richly glazed flowerpots, vases, and wall flower holders, as well as large urns for yard display. These were often marked and had applied decoration, both cast and hand-formed.

Pennsylvania craftsmen produced similar pieces as well as the peculiar Bolle Kasse, or bulb planters, ovoid vases with holes in the sides. These held onions that would sprout through the holes and then be snipped off for use in cooking. Both Bolle Kasse and flowerpots might have received a variety of decoration including sgraffito, coggling, slip, and stamp work, reflecting the fact that these humble objects were often given as gifts. Such pieces were made to order and could be relatively expensive. On the other hand, the unglazed gallon flowerpots sold in 1864 by the Norwalk, Connecticut, pottery cost only $1.80 per dozen. Glazed examples were just $.20 more.

TOYS AND MINIATURES

Redware toys were made in some quantity and over a long period of time. The Manhattan craftsman Dirck Claesen produced them in the 1660s, and two hundred years later the A. E.

A group of manganese-glazed miniatures only 2½ to 3 inches high. Most such pieces are attributed to Pennsylvania. All date c. 1840–80.

Smith Pottery at Norwalk, Connecticut, was offering "toy cups and dishes" at fifteen cents per dozen.

The variety of such items found is surprising, and it is not clear what all were used for. There seems little doubt that tiny cups and saucers were made as playthings and in imitation of contemporary white earthenware and porcelain examples. The bird-shaped water whistles and rattles so popular among Pennsylvania craftsmen were also undoubtedly toys.

However, there exist many well-formed miniatures of redware jugs, jars, vases, pitchers, pots, chamber pots, molds, and even rundlets. Some have claimed that these are salesmen's samples designed to display a potter's skill and versatility. There is, however, no written evidence or reminiscence to support this theory.

From the quantity that survive, one may suspect that these tiny objects served a variety of uses. Some were toys. Some, such as the miniature jugs turned at early-twentieth-century fairs by the Fort Edward, New York, potters Alexander and Frederick Hilfinger, were novelty items or souvenirs of a visit to the kiln. Certainly some were collected for mantel dis-

play, just as Victorians acquired similar pieces in porcelain.

Most miniature redware is either unglazed or covered with a black or clear-lead slip. Rarest and most sought after are examples in several colors and those with incised names and dates.

Dolls and doll heads of conventional size are known, though rare. The master potter at Salem, North Carolina, c. 1821–43, John Frederic Holland, listed four types of "dolls" in his inventories, priced at five, eight, ten, and fifteen cents each. These were actually slip-cast heads that could be attached to a cloth body. The Moravian potters also made small dolls as well as other toys a few inches long, including dogs, chickens, geese, and lions. Doll heads and clay animals were also produced in Pennsylvania and in the Strasburg area of Virginia.

Dollhouse furniture, hand- or slab-built and including such items as chairs, tables, cupboards, couches, and even dressers, is extremely rare. Much more common are marbles, both glazed and unglazed. Though probably made at every shop, they are seldom mentioned in inventories.

There were even a few toy musical instruments, particularly the tabor, a simple two-hole instrument resembling a flute or recorder, and the ocarina or "sweet potato." Few of these have survived.

Penny Banks

Another item designed primarily for children was the penny bank, or money jug, as it was termed in many pottery price lists. Most commonly these were acorn- or ball-shaped and often left unglazed so that they might be decorated by their young owners. Such banks were offered in 1864 at forty cents per dozen by the Norwalk, Connecticut, pottery. The Caire Pottery at Huntington, New York, listed them around the same time at thirty-seven and a half cents for twelve, indicating close competition

Lead-glazed redware penny bank cast in the form of an Empire chest of drawers, Pennsylvania, c. 1860–90. Such quaint examples usually date to the late nineteenth century.

bottles. Though occasionally assayed by New England and midwestern craftsmen, this was almost exclusively the province of North Carolina, Virginia, and Pennsylvania potters.

Bottles and Flasks

Smaller whiskey flasks assumed many and surprising shapes, particularly among the Moravians of North Carolina. Best-known of their examples is the green-glazed standing squirrel bottle, sold in 1820 at one or two shillings, depending on size. Other typical Moravian forms included the bear, listed in the 1810 inventory; the fox, which clutches a chicken in its paws; three birds—the eagle, goose, and owl; and several forms of aquatic life. Among these are a fish, a turtle (the first figural bottle listed in Moravian inventories, in 1800), and a crawfish.

Decades later, the kilns in the Shenandoah Valley turned out their own unusual vessels including one shaped like a potato; a gemel or double bottle by Solomon Bell that featured two men standing back to back, each with mug in hand; and a flask in the form of a pig.

Other human forms include, from Pennsylvania, a bottle in the guise of a woman with hands on hips, and a rare, Poughkeepsie, New York, flask in the shape of a standing man.

Mantel Decorations

Inspired by imported Staffordshire novelties, Virginia and Pennsylvania potters turned out an array of decorative figures. Dogs were especially popular. Among the most desirable are the re-

between the two neighboring shops. Among the few marked examples are banks by Willoughby Smith of Womelsdorf, Pennsylvania.

There were also more elaborate money jugs. Some were cast in molds to resemble furniture such as an Empire chest of drawers. Pennsylvania examples might be hand-built in the form of an owl's head or a jar slip-glazed and decorated with pierced and punch work and surmounted by an animal such as a dog or rooster.

Perhaps the most remarkable penny banks are the unglazed redware compositions created by the potter John G. Schweinfurt of New Market, Virginia. Turned and hand-molded, one of these consists of a kilnlike structure with four chimneys, atop which a boy kneels before the penny slot. A pigeon tops the spire above his head and an intricate braided handle serves both as a lift and a unifying element.

FIGURAL PIECES

Though seldom seen for sale or in most collections, there is a variety of figural redware. Humans, animals, birds, and fish appear. Some examples were designed as mantelpiece ornaments, like the popular Staffordshire figurines, others as doorstops, and still others as novelty

Figurine in the form of a standing ram, lead-glazed redware, Pennsylvania, c. 1850–80. Such decorative pieces mimic English Staffordshire mantelpiece figures.

Again in the Staffordshire manner, dogs, often Spaniels, served as doorstops. Usually molded or hand-built, these were made at the Galena, Illinois, pottery and were glazed in rich yellows and browns. In Ohio, redware dogs were often given a brown Albany-slip finish. Unglazed examples were painted by the customer.

Plaques

A few ornamental plaques with molded relief decoration are known, among them one of a woman beside a fig tree that was done by the Eberly Pottery of Virginia as an advertisement for the Fig Syrup Company.

MISCELLANEOUS WARES

There are quite a few redware objects that fall into no particular general category. Some, such as stovepipes, were made by many potteries; others, like beehives, are great rarities.

Inkstands, Inkwells, and Sanders

Since education was prized in the developing society, items associated with literacy were often given an added decorative touch. The inkstand, an oblong piece that combined wells for different colored inks with penholders and sanders, was the most elaborate. An unusual example marked by John Bell and made at the Winchester, Virginia, pottery of Peter Bell is slip-decorated in blue on an opaque white ground, in imitation of European delftware. Pennsylvania inkstands were often decorated with pierced work and embellished with animal or bird forms.

More modest, round inkwells might simply have a central hole for dipping and several smaller ones for quill pens. All would, however,

clining whippets produced and marked by several members of the Bell clan, Solomon, Samuel, and Richard F., all of Strasburg, Virginia. Other forms include dogs standing, sitting on their haunches, and carrying baskets. Few are ever marked, but most are glazed, sometimes quite elaborately. Though some such pieces were cast in molds, most were hand-built. Sizes range from four to ten inches.

Lions, sometimes for use as bookends, were also popular, as were squirrels, deer, bears (one piece by Baecher of Strasburg features a mother bear holding a cub), roosters, sheep, cats, and human figures. The human figures might be in the classical Victorian mode—pretty boys and girls holding baskets of flowers—or much earthier, like a man sitting on a stump holding a whiskey jug or another playing the fiddle with his dog at his knee. Some of these pieces also had a practical use. Hollow figures served as vases or toothpick holders, while a horse and rider bore a basket on each side that held bottles of oil and vinegar, thus doubling as a castor set.

Heart-shaped redware inkwell with slip decoration in yellow, Connecticut, c. 1790–1810. Such an elaborate piece was probably a gift or love token.

be glazed, usually in lead or manganese, but often in several colors. Turned spool-shaped sanders held the white sand used in blotting a freshly written page. They were usually given a clear or black finish. John Vickers of Chester County, Pennsylvania, sold them in 1834 for only two cents apiece!

Watch Hutches

In many early homes the only timepiece was father's pocket watch, which at night would be placed in a box-shaped ceramic receptacle with a hole through which the watch face could be seen, thus creating a miniature clock. Redware hutches are rare. One of the finest examples, slab-thrown and decorated before glazing with floral and animal motifs and rope-twist columns, bears the incised signature of Anthony Baecher, "journey man potter," and was made in Pennsylvania before he established his shop in Virginia.

Redware inkwells: left, Ohio, c. 1860–80; right, Maine, c. 1830–45. Inkwells were made in surprising quantity and variety.

Stoves and Stovepipes

Heating stoves of cast iron and baked tile were made in Central Europe throughout the 1700s, and it is likely that any German-trained potter would be familiar with them. Yet, only in two places do we find documentary evidence of their manufacture. The first is North Carolina, where several eighteenth-century Moravian-made examples still exist. The other is Bergholz, New York, where, a century later, the German immigrant potter Carl Mehwaldt produced similar pieces. Since the Moravians came to North Carolina from Pennsylvania, it is likely that the stoves were made there as well.

In all cases the stove tiles were press- or slip-molded. Some were used in the bisque state after being heavily covered with stove polish. Others were glazed in green or yellow-brown tortoise-shell.

The feet of regular cast-iron stoves often rested on ceramic footrests, insulating them from contact with the wooden floor. Such rests were circular and had a rimmed depression at the top to hold the stove foot. Most were plain and unglazed, but one will encounter fancily turned specimens in manganese or multicolored glaze. They were made, of course, in sets of four.

Stovepipe collars, also known as "thimbles" and referred to in most price lists as "stove tubes," were cylindrical pieces of unglazed redware used to insulate walls from hot sheet-iron stovepipes. Though rarely marked or otherwise identified, they were made by most shops. Peter Bell of Hagerstown, Maryland, sold two sizes, at $.12½ and $.25 each in 1808; and in the 1880s Fulper Brothers of Flemington, New Jersey, asked $2.25 per dozen for their twelve-inch version. Roof exits were insulated with chimney tops that sold at $1.50 *apiece*, a reflection of their large size. These may still be seen on house tops in rural Pennsylvania.

Roofing Tiles

Also found atop the house were unglazed shield-shaped roof tiles. These were referred to in early inventories as "pantiles," and were a common product of Dutch and German potters. How important a part of the business they might be is reflected in the fact that when, in 1788, the Manhattan Common Council forbade further removal of clay from public lands, the New York potter John Campbell protested that "unless he be permitted to procure clay there his manufactory of pantiles must cease." Apparently, something was worked out, because Campbell remained in business until nearly 1800.

After 1850, redware potters were more likely to make drainage tile used in farming. These semicircular pieces or "horseshoe" tiles were first made over wooden molds, but by the 1860s most shops were employing machinery for the task.

Redware roof tile, patented 1871 by James B. Hamilton, Greensboro, Pennsylvania. Most roof tiles are unmarked and unidentifiable. This example may be traced through patent records to a Pennsylvania firm.

Two pipes, one unglazed, the other slipped in a gray-white; both date c. 1850–80. Since pipe-head making required only a small mold and kiln, many artisans confined themselves to this limited branch of the potter's trade.

Smoking Pipe Bowls

On a more personal level, most potters turned out redware bowls for long-stemmed pipes. These were pressed in small molds and baked in special ovens. Many were in the shape of human or animal heads. Both glazed and unglazed examples are known. To give one an idea of the volume in which these were made, the Wachovia, North Carolina, kilns produced 3,200 dozen in the year 1808 alone.

Cane Heads

Similar molds were used to manufacture cane heads that could be fitted to wooden canes. Remaining examples take the form of birds, animals, and human heads. Either there was a high rate of attrition or cane users didn't fancy this item, since few specimens have survived.

Birdhouses and Birdbaths

Insect-eating birds were valued by farmers, and ceramic birdhouses were an early product of American shops. The remains of one of these bottle-shaped havens were found at the eighteenth-century Yorktown pottery site.

There were two general types: martin houses or "boxes" that looked like large jars with an opening at one end and air-hole perforations in the side; and beehive-shaped, dome-topped wren boxes with a small entrance hole and clay perch on the side. The former were made and glazed in brown by the Solomon Bell pottery of Strasburg, Virginia; while Henry Schofield of Rock Springs, Maryland, was making the latter as late as 1943.

Shallow, platelike birdbaths of unglazed redware were also made by some potteries, as were poultry waterers that were turned to resemble a handleless jug and had a traylike receptacle at the base into which water flowed. A marked, unglazed example by Austin Hempstead who worked in Queens County, New York, is known, as well as unmarked ones in clear and yellow slip glaze.

Beehives

A great oddity is the unglazed redware beehive in the collection of the Pennsylvania Farm Museum. Turned on a wheel, this large (twelve-by-fifteen-inch) piece imitated in form but apparently not in function the common nineteenth-century rye straw bee skeps. It appears to be an idea whose time never came.

Roach Traps

A less useful insect is the roach, and potters did their bit in the unceasing war against this pest. Their contribution was a round well-like receptacle with an unglazed ridged exterior (to facilitate the bugs' entry) and a sloping, overhung glazed rim. The bugs followed the scent of molasses or some other sweet up the sides and down into the well from whence they were unable to emerge.

Picture Frames

Picture frames were a necessity in the Victorian home, and some potters, particularly in Virginia, tried to accommodate the demand. Molded frames in the shape of foliate ovals surmounted by an eagle were made and marked at Strasburg, Virginia, by Samuel Bell. Like Bell pitchers, they were often glazed in brown and green on a cream ground.

Doorknobs and Furniture Knobs

It is likely that quite a few shops tried their hands at redware doorknobs and chest knobs, sponging redware with brown or black in imitation of the Rockingham knobs so popular in the mid-nineteenth century. Among the few firms known to have actually sold these wares is that of James Quintard at Norwalk, Connecticut, c. 1825–40.

Buttons

Buttons were another little-known product of the redware craftsman; and, again, we must thank the Quintard firm for what little we know of this interesting item. Examples traced to this firm resemble (as they were no doubt supposed to) the tortoiseshell and bone buttons commonly used on Victorian clothing.

Umbrella Stands

Large umbrella stands were made from Maine to Virginia and Ohio. Many were left unglazed so that they might be decorated by amateur artists. Others, especially the products of the late-nineteenth-century Shenandoah kilns, were lavishly slipped and decorated with sprigged and hand-built decorative elements.

Coffins and Tombstones

The potter's efforts might even follow one to the grave. In some areas of the South, baked redware coffins or crematory urns were preferred, and tombstones were manufactured from the same material, thus completing the cycle begun with the pap bowl or baby feeder.

3

MASSACHUSETTS

THE BIRTHPLACE of New England redware potting was undoubtedly Massachusetts. Every known seventeenth-century craftsman came from here, and of the three hundred or so potters working in the New England area prior to 1800, almost 90 percent were active in the Bay State.

Moreover, it was here that English ceramic traditions held sway. Dutch and German artisans, common farther south, were rare; and both form and decoration reflected British preferences. These were by nature conservative, and they became more so with the hardships both potters and their customers endured in the new land. Laura Woodside Watkins, whose monumental *Early New England Potters and Their Wares* remains, forty years after publication, the definitive book on New England ceramics, has argued persuasively that limitations on decoration imposed by early living conditions became traditional after 1800, resulting in wares that seem somber compared with the sgraffito work of Pennsylvania or the splashy glazes and applied decoration of Virginia.

It should not be assumed, though, that early English decoration was drab. Wares made there in the seventeenth and eighteenth centuries were characterized by exuberant trailed-slip patterns and the use of natural coloring agents to produce a rainbow of hues: red, yellow, brown, green, white, and black.

Despite the fact that many of these colorants were difficult to obtain or expensive in the New World, Watkins's excavations during the 1930s and 1940s revealed that at least some of the Massachusetts potters attempted to mimic English decoration. At Danvers she explored the sherd pile of James Kettle (c. 1687–1710), finding not only the usual dome-shaped lard pots (clear-glazed only on the interior) but also fragments of bowls and deep dishes decorated with slip-trailed loops and r-shaped devices in white, some of which were further embellished by drippings of green copper oxide.

Even stronger evidence of the decorative nature of early Massachusetts wares was uncovered at Newburyport, where from 1764 to 1799

Early ovoid redware jug with mottled glaze, Massachusetts or New Hampshire, c. 1820–40. The graceful form and early handle attachment mark this piece as superior.

two generations of the Bayley family worked. Daniel Bayley, whose father had also been a potter in the town, bought a house there in 1763; and by the following year he had built a shop and kiln. Within three years of his death in 1796, the little factory was shut down never to be used again. Thus, Watkins was able to date the large quantity of sherds that she found to a single thirty-six-year period.

The list of identified forms was an imposing one, indicating the importance of an eighteenth-century potter to his community. Bowls, milk or bread pans, baking and deep dishes, pudding pans, porringers, several types of mugs, teapots, beakers, pitchers, jugs, chambers, and, of course, the ubiquitous lard pots were among the finds.

The majority of these were glazed only on the interior; but mugs in solid manganese as well as orange-streaked on brown were found. Pitchers varied in hue from rose to light green. Bowls were finished in a dripped greenish brown or in mahogany with a bright orange interior or banded about the rim in a pale tan slip, a technique similar to that being then employed at some English kilns. Porringers, deep dishes, and chamber pots were sometimes brushed with light slip in random patterns or, with the dishes, concentric circles or scalloping about the interior. The initials *WB* even appeared upon one dish. None of these pieces can be said to be particularly sophisticated or comparable to work that was being done in England at the same period, but the sheer variety of color and decoration is most impressive.

Another interesting aspect of Watkins's digging at the Bayley site was that she also was able to examine two other properties where members of the family had worked, at Rowley and Gloucester, thus extending the period of her observation to seventy-seven years, from 1720 to 1799. What she discovered was that neither form nor decoration changed significantly over this period, nor did the fragments found vary much from those excavated at other pottery sites of the same period. What this tells us is, as I have indicated elsewhere, that it is extremely difficult to date American redware solely on the basis of form. Tradition and resistance to change were the norm; innovation the exception.

An interesting aspect of the potters' craft is the apprenticeship system, and this is illustrated in the life of another Newburyport craftsman,

Ebenezer Morrison. An orphan, Ebenezer, at the age of thirteen, was assigned to work for the potter Stephen Kent under articles that were, to say the least, limiting. The Agreement of November 26, 1754, provided that he serve seven and a half years, obey his master and mistress, neither waste their possessions or suffer others to do so, keep their secrets, and labor honestly at his work. Hardly unreasonable, particularly for the time; but the agreement *also* provided that Morrison could not leave the house without permission, visit taverns, alehouses, or the theater, play dice or cards, or "commit fornication" or marry within the period of his servitude. The good news is that Ebenezer put in his time, married almost immediately thereafter, opened his own pot shop, and, eventually, became successful.

THE POTTERS BY PERIOD

As one might suspect, the earliest known Massachusetts potters were located in and around Boston, particularly at Charlestown, then a separate community. Philip Drinker is the first. He arrived from England in 1635 on the ship *Abigail*, and when he died in 1647, he left behind evidence of his occupation in a will that conveyed the "house I now live in with the kiln and garden . . . with all the tools belonging to my trade. . . ." Drinker's son, Edward, carried on the business until 1655 when he was forced to flee to Boston to escape persecution for his religious beliefs. There he operated a successful shop until his death in 1700. There does not appear to have been another potter active in Bos-

ton proper until David Simons arrived in 1748. He remained at work until 1766.

Other nearby settlements were also popular with ceramic craftsmen. The kilns of William Vinson or Vincent (c. 1635–45) and John Pride (c. 1635–47) were located at Salem, while the previously mentioned James Kettle worked at Beverly and Danvers (c. 1685–1710); Jonathan Hayward was also in Beverly from 1694 to 1733. Dorchester was another important site with Joseph, David, and Peletiah Hall carrying on a thriving trade from 1733 to 1777.

But it was at Charlestown that the business really developed. Another Kettle, Samuel, went there in 1665 to take over the trade that Edward Drinker had abandoned and established a shop run by his family for a full century. However, he was not without competition. During the early decades of the eighteenth century some forty potters were active in the town, and the term *Charlestown Ware* became synonymous with redware. Sad to say, none of this great production can be identified with certainty today.

Among the better-known craftsmen were Isaac Parker and his son, John (c. 1714–57); Daniel Edes (c. 1726–64), John Harris (c. 1746–69), Thomas Symmes (c. 1726–44), Josiah Harris (c. 1745–86), and Jonathan Penney (c. 1763–75).

John Parker left behind a fascinating day book that detailed his activities as a potter for the period from 1747 to 1757; while Thomas Symmes advertised in 1744 that he made "red and yellow Ware of divers sorts," an indication that slip decoration was being practiced here, too.

During its heyday from about 1740 until 1775, Charlestown was a ceramic boomtown with wares being shipped up the coast as far as Casco Bay, Maine, and as far south as central Connecticut. However, storm clouds loomed. By 1741, the threat of fire (a constant around pot shops) and objection to the noxious smoke emitted by the kilns had caused the General Court to pass an act "[f]or preventing of deso-

---

◄ *Ovoid two-handled (one missing) jar or vase, Massachusetts, c. 1780–1800. The heavily ringed neck and freestanding handles are typical of the earliest American redware.*

lation by fire, that may happen by erecting of potters' kilns & houses near to dwelling-houses and other buildings & the inconvenience and mischief that may accrue to the neighborhood by the offensive and unwholesome smoak & stench proceeding from the kilns when on fire. . . ." (Laura Woodside Watkins, *Early New England Potters and Their Wares* [Hamden, Ct.: Archon Books, 1968].)

Just what effect this bill, which was essentially designed to license and limit the building of potteries, had on the trade is unknown; but the next blow to business was a more substantial one. In 1775, English troops burned Charlestown and its earthenware factories to the ground. Only one potter, Battery Powers (c. 1758–1807), survived the fire. He was later joined by John Runey (c. 1788–1829), whose family continued his business until around 1860; but Charlestown's earthenware makers never recovered, in part due to the fact that the trade moved north and west following people who were migrating into more sparsely settled areas of the state.

Danvers, where James Kettle had toiled, was the most important ceramics center north of Boston. Twenty-two young potters from the Danvers-Peabody area fought in the Battle of Lexington, and during the period of 1775 to 1825 there were thirty-three different pot shops that employed dozens of craftsmen, of whom some thirty bore the name Osborn.

The first of these was Joseph Osborn, who founded a business in 1736 that was run by his sons and grandsons until 1853. One son, Amos, worked at his own kiln from the late eighteenth century until his death in 1836. His shop passed through various hands until purchased in 1876 by Moses B. Paige, who operated it well into the present century.

Though other names—Southwick, Wilson, Purinton, and Goldthwaite—occur among the potters of Danvers, the Osborns were dominant. Moreover, from here family apprentices went out to found potteries in other Massachu-

setts towns, as well as in New Hampshire, Maine, New York, and Rhode Island.

But as is so often the case in Massachusetts, where redware was rarely ever marked, it is extremely difficult to identify Danvers ware. There is a black-glazed mug found in the chimney of Joseph Osborn's old house and thus reasonably attributed to his shop, a miniature jug made at the family pottery in 1828 for another Osborn, Abraham C., and a variety of pieces owned by local museums and historical societies—all with somewhat tenuous attributions. Watkins felt that no slip-decorated wares were made here, and that the characteristic color scheme was orange-red brushed with brown.

Other northern communities could also boast of redware shops. The seventeenth-century kilns at Salem were succeeded by Nathaniel Symonds and his descendants, active from 1740 until 1820; while Abraham Annis worked at Haverhill (c. 1737–50), John West (c. 1767–81) at Bradford, and John Proctor (c. 1766–1805) at

An early manganese-glazed mug, probably Massachusetts, c. 1800–20, which lost its handle years ago and was recycled as a tea caddy. Collectors call such items "make-dos."

Redware spittoon in yellow slip splashed with brown, New England or New York, c. 1830–50. An attractive finish adds value to what is normally a modestly priced piece.

(c. 1740–80) was run by Paul Osborn, yet one more of that prolific clan, and Edward Shove, scion of another important Massachusetts potting family. Allied by marriage and both of the Quaker faith, the Osborn and Shove families collaborated in a variety of enterprises in Bristol County.

Even longer-lasting businesses were established at Freetown by William Boyce and heirs (c. 1799–1885) and at Somerset where Clark Purinton built a kiln in 1753. In an area then known as Pottersville, three generations of his family made earthenware until 1835. Excavation of the site has revealed that vessels produced there were slip-decorated and spattered or dotted in green in a manner remarkably similar to that employed by the Bayleys at Newburyport.

Another of the Pottersville craftsmen was Asa Chase (c. 1782–1812), best-known as the master with whom Elija Cornell served his apprenticeship. Cornell, who later worked in New York State, was the father of Ezra, founder of Cornell University.

West of Boston there were several active potteries in Worcester County, the most important located in the Brookfield area, home to Charles Bailey (c. 1770–1800), Elisha Drake (c. 1800–23) and Samuel Stevens (c. 1815–37). The latter carried Massachusetts traditions to Michigan in the 1840s. At a much later date (c. 1879–88) Richard Linley and Abner S. Wright had a sizable factory in East Brookfield. They made the ordinary flowerpots and redware, but also are known to have turned out small banks in the form of apples, oranges, and pears. Such pieces are sometimes encountered in antiques shops,

Gloucester, from whence ships carried his wares "from Maine to Virginia." A much later factory was run by Charles A. Lawrence at Beverly (c. 1866–1906). Early products included attractive vessels brushed in green and white on a tan ground, but in later years only flowerpots and the usual terra-cotta "art wares" were produced.

There was even some activity at the little town of Merrimacport, hard by the New Hampshire border. Benjamin Bodge, who began work here in 1775, sold his pottery in 1791. He was followed by William Pecker, whose identified work consists of several lovely ovoid vessels splashed with dark brown upon a light reddish orange ground. Pecker was active at least as early as 1784, probably as an employee of Bodge, and died in 1820, crushed to death in the collapse of his kiln—an end, along with fire and explosion, all too common among early potters.

Pecker's nephew, James Chase, took over the Merrimacport business carrying on until 1849, when it passed to his son, Phineas, who ran it through 1864. Though there are rumors of green-glazed wares, the only identifiable examples from the Chase manufactory are ordinary pans and bean pots glazed only on the interior.

South of Boston, toward Rhode Island, there were several potteries at Taunton. The earliest

Two redware penny banks in the form of apples, attributed to East Brookfield, Mass., c. 1879–88. Also shaped like peaches, pears, and oranges, these banks were painted after firing rather than glazed.

but this is the only New England shop identified with their production.

Contemporary records also indicate that the Shaker settlement at Shirley, Massachusetts (c. 1793–1909), produced pipe bowls, one William Bentley noting in his diary for July 19, 1795, that "[w]e were invited to smoak & some pipes of their own casting were brought. They were of clay, & the stems called stails were of osier. . . ."

In Worcester proper, Joseph Thorp and Jonathan Nash ran a pottery (c. 1773–84); while, to the north of the city, in West Sterling, was the Wachusett Pottery established by Henry Tolman sometime between 1820 and 1837. By 1849 Tolman's son, Henry Jr., was in charge in partnership with Abner S. Wight, who bought the concern in 1860. By 1869 Marcus L. Snow, with several partners, was the owner, and he operated the business until 1881.

The important thing about the Wachusett Pottery was that it came as close to being a factory on the order of contemporary stoneware shops as did any Massachusetts redware kiln. In the 1870s, around fifteen men were regularly employed, and wares were sold throughout the Northeast. Moreover, molds, more commonly associated with the production of yellow and white earthenware, were extensively employed; and an 1853 bill head offered "Fancy Pressed Ware with Rockingham Glaze."

Watkins's exploration of the old kiln site revealed that what was made here was not a true Rockingham, which has a yellow earthen (or white if English) body, but redware covered with a dark brown glaze. Similiar wares are known to have been made in Pennsylvania and, particularly, in Canada.

In the far western part of the state, Thomas Goldthwaite of Danvers ran a pottery at Springfield (c. 1763–76), while Jonathan Hall was active in South Hadley (c. 1767–73) and Northampton (c. 1773–76), where he was succeeded by Deacon Ebenezer Hunt (c. 1779–

1800), a nonpotter who employed several workmen and raised a large establishment.

None, though, was more successful than the potters of Whately, a town about ten miles from Northampton, who started with redware and then transferred their efforts to making stoneware. The earliest shop was that of Jonathan Pierce (c. 1778), but Stephen Orcutt, who went into business before 1797, is remembered as the town's first stoneware manufacturer, a field he embarked upon soon after 1800. Orcutt's sons, Eleazer and Walter, are well known to pottery collectors, having been involved in numerous stoneware- and redware-making ventures at various locations throughout New York, Maine, and Massachusetts.

Another important Whately potter was Thomas Crafts (c. 1806–48). Seizing upon an idea introduced about 1820 by the Troy, New York, potter Sanford S. Perry, Crafts began the manufacture of black-glazed teapots in 1821. Excavation has revealed that some of these were wheel-turned while others were cast in the manner of New Jersey and Pennsylvania examples. Crafts continued this business for a decade, apparently with great success, until turning to stoneware. Interestingly enough, most of his output was sold not in the vicinity or even in the state, but was shipped to New York City and Philadelphia. Crafts's teapots were not marked, but may be tentatively identified through sherds excavated at Whately.

It is from this shop also that one of the two marked pieces of nineteenth-century Massachusetts redware comes. It is a milk pan impressed on the base: T. CRAFTS. The other known example is also a milk pan. It is stamped F. T. WRIGHT & CO./STONEWARE/TAUNTON. It is regrettable that more of the state's rich earthenware heritage was not so identified.

4

NEW HAMPSHIRE AND VERMONT

THOUGH NEIGHBORS, the states of New Hampshire and Vermont developed quite different redware industries. The proximity of the former to Boston assured early settlement as well as frequent trade, and potters from Massachusetts were active in the state early in the eighteenth century, laying the foundation for pottery-making operations that in some cases lasted into the late 1800s. The isolation of Vermont, on the other hand, prevented the growth of earthenware potteries until a time when stoneware became available; and the latter quickly occupied the market.

For the most part, redware made in these states is quite similar in its conservative form and particularly in its decoration. Though Massachusetts craftsmen, and to a lesser extent those from Connecticut, dominated the field in both states, they seem to have left behind their more exuberant instincts. The famed slip script of the Connecticut Valley is nowhere to be found, and the splashy glazes of Massachusetts are greatly

toned down once they cross the northern borders. Here, utility is the prime consideration.

NEW HAMPSHIRE

Though short, the New Hampshire coastline provides an important opening to the world, and it was along this strand that the first indigenous potteries were established. Henry Moulton was working at Sandown c. 1720–63; and Samuel Marshall (1729–49) was the first potter in the important seafaring town of Portsmouth. Little is known of their products, though, at his death, Marshall left behind a "Parcel of Earthenware" and "Potter's Working Gear" or tools, the latter valued at the substantial sum of seventeen pounds.

Exeter, however, was the most important early center, and it was there that the Massachusetts craftsman Jabez Dodge set up shop in 1771. A large milk pan decorated with bands of

A pair of the small preserve pots often called apple-butter jars or pots. One is clear-lead-glazed, the other glazed only on the interior. Both are from the northeastern United States and date c. 1840–1900.

light and dark slip and bearing the inscription "DMA/1830" is attributed to this kiln. It is one of the very few known examples of New Hampshire slip decoration. Other than for this, Exeter products appear to have been rather conservative: common forms given a clear lead glaze with occasional touches of manganese.

The Dodge Pottery was continued by Jabez's son Samuel through 1849 and then until 1895 by members of the Lamson family, potters who had married into the Dodge line. Many craftsmen who later worked in Maine or in Vermont got their training here; and portions of the second pottery building, set up in 1819, now form part of the ceramics display at Greenfield Village and Henry Ford Museum in Dearborn, Michigan.

Joseph, another son of Jabez Dodge, moved to nearby Portsmouth where he and later his sons worked from 1804 to at least 1851. The Portsmouth operation was a relatively large one. The industrial census of 1830 indicates that it employed four men and turned out $1,200 worth of redware, a substantial figure for the time.

As the interior was developed, New Hamp-

Manganese-splashed preserve jar, New England or Pennsylvania, c. 1830–70. Vessels such as these were made over a wide area and can seldom be specifically identified.

shire potters moved inland, establishing an important center at Chesham or "Pottersville" near Dublin. By 1812 nearly a dozen small shops were operating in this area, encouraged, no doubt, by the war that cut off access to English and Continental ceramics. Among the names that have come down to us are Jedediah Southwick (c. 1809–43), John Wight and son (1845–66), and Eben and Osgood Russell (c. 1840–60).

An 1850s price list from the Russell shop indicates that it was producing the usual redware forms: a variety of pots, bread and baking pans, preserve jars, pitchers, jugs, pie plates, bowls, chambers, and, of course, flowerpots. Examples attributed to the Chesham kilns are frequently glazed in an attractive green or given an overall manganese finish. The former is uncommon elsewhere in New England, but black glaze was employed throughout the area.

Another important locality was Lyndeborough or Lyndboro, west of Exeter and well inland. In 1775 Peter Clark, also a Massachusetts potter and from Braintree, set up shop here; and with his sons Daniel, Peter, and William, he operated several small kilns, the last of which burned in 1851. Yellow-green and brown are the colors most commonly found on their wares. One of the very few pieces of marked New Hampshire redware is associated with this site, a bulbous lead-glazed jug inscribed MADE BY DANIEL CLARK IN LYNDEBOROUGH DURING THE YEAR 1792.

It was in this year that Daniel moved from Lyndeborough to the expanding community of Concord, where he built a small shop and oven. His grandson John ran the shop until 1885. There is another unusual piece associated with this pottery, a brown-glazed plate with incised

---

◀ Ovoid preserve jar with matching top, probably New Hampshire, c. 1830–50. Excellent form and an appealing glaze in an essentially utilitarian piece.

concentric rim decoration and the inscription "Concord September th 12-1807."

The Concord factory turned out a variety of wares. In the earlier days there were the customary creamers, sugar bowls, jugs, pots, and jars, as well as less common pieces such as the hard-to-throw rundlet. After the Civil War, flowerpots and unglazed "art ware" of various sorts occupied the workers' time. Perhaps the most unusual of these to survive is a slab-constructed miniature log cabin of the type most often seen in Pennsylvania and Virginia.

The New Hampshire decoration most popular with contemporary collectors is a mottled, usually orange-green, glaze said to have been produced at the pottery established in Gonic by Elijah Osborne. Active from 1839 until 1885 in the small town near Rochester, the Osborne Pottery produced typical earthenware products, none of which appear to have been marked. The eagerness with which mottled wares are attributed to it is more a reflection of wishful thinking than the result of sound analysis.

Jeremiah Burpee, best-known of nineteenth-century New Hampshire craftsmen, operated a pottery at Boscawen, north of Concord, from 1804 until his death in 1862. The usual jars, jugs, and pots were here embellished with a clear or yellow slip glaze and with tooled decorations in the form of scallops, beading, or wavy lines. Typically, Burpee's ware would be egg-shaped with a swollen midpoint below which the pieces would be left unglazed. The general feeling is one of delicacy, reflecting the fine touch of the potter.

Farther north, at the edge of the White Mountains, is West Plymouth, a tiny community that for years supplied most of the ceramic needs of wild northern New Hampshire. The potter Peter Flanders established himself here in 1807, and with his son maintained a lively business until 1869. However, the Flanderses were not without competition. Daniel D. Webster was active in the town from 1817 until his death in

Large ovoid storage jar with a lovely, rich, and flowing light tan glaze, New Hampshire, c. 1810–30. The egg-shaped form characterizes many early pieces.

1832, and other members of the family continued the trade; though in later years they appear to have been employed by William and John Gill, who opened the third Plymouth shop in 1830, maintaining it until 1886.

Of all these, only the work of the Gills is known. They, too, produced mottled orange-green ware including the tall stew pots that are typical of both Maine and New Hampshire.

Though there are reports of kilns being established farther north, successful earthenware manufacture appears to have been limited to the area south of Lake Winnipesaukee. West of here and not far from Hanover, Isaac Lowell built a pottery at Canaan in 1818. Three generations of the family fired this oven until it was shut down

in 1872. In 1869, a son, Elijah, made three black-glazed pieces—a porringer, a cup, and a jug—as gifts. Now owned by the New Hampshire Historical Society, these are the only remaining examples from the shop.

Latest of all the New Hampshire redware factories but also the best-known among collectors is that established in 1871 at Keene by J. S. Taft and Company. The Tafts started out making the usual redware, but they soon became caught up in the Victorian craze for art pottery (something that would have been regarded as useless by the pragmatic New Hampshire farmer), producing various patterns and glazes until 1916. "Hampshire" pottery, as it is now termed, is among the favorites of contemporary collectors.

That this should have been the last and one of the most successful of the New Hampshire potteries is ironic. Plain and practical were always the way in New Hampshire.

VERMONT

Given its isolation and lack of seacoast, one might reasonably suppose that the Vermont redware industry would develop gradually along the Massachusetts and New Hampshire borders, as craftsmen moved north or west into the forested highlands. Actually, though, the first potters seem to have headed directly north toward the Canadian border.

Isaac Brown Farrar of New Ipswich, New Hampshire, established a kiln at Fairfax, Vermont (northeast of Burlington and within thirty miles of Canada) c. 1798, laying the foundation for a dynasty of potters who made both redware and stoneware not only here and in Burlington, but also in Galesville, Syracuse, Seneca Falls, and North Bay, New York, and at several Canadian locations. The Farrars, whose history remains largely unexplored, were one of the most important families of early American potters, rivaling the Nortons and the Bells in significance. Yet, nothing seems to be known of the redware they produced at Fairfax; and by 1840 they were running a thriving stoneware factory there.

One member of the clan, however, never abandoned the earthenware business. Caleb Farrar opened a redware shop in Middlebury in 1812 and ran it until 1850. He made the customary forms—jugs, jars, pots, and bowls—enhancing their appearance with lead glazes tinted in shades of rose, yellow, and pale green.

Another early settler, this one from Massachusetts, was potter Charles Bailey, who settled in Hardwick, northwest of St. Johnsbury, soon after 1772. Though he may have worked as late as 1840, nothing is known of his output. Then, Moses Bradley came from Haverhill, Massa-

chusetts, to Chimney Point on the western border at Lake Champlain. He worked there from 1790 until 1797, when he moved his operations to West Woodstock, where he continued through 1824.

Bradley appears to have been a popular local figure, particularly interesting to the children of Woodstock. An elderly resident was quoted in Henry Swan Dana's *History of Woodstock, Vermont* (1889) as having as a child "stood silently by him a great many hours and watched him, while from a lump of clay put upon the wheel he would draw up a structure which would turn out to be a vase, a pitcher or a jug."

Peter Clark, Jr., of the Lyndeborough, New Hampshire, family, worked at Barton in eastern Vermont from 1798 until sometime before 1813, when he returned to his native town and was replaced in Barton by a potter named Samuel Ward. And another Massachusetts craftsman, Samuel Woodman, settled at Poultney, southwest of Rutland and close to the New York line in 1800. He was succeeded by his son, John, in 1820. It is not known how long the shop remained in operation after that.

An 1814 entry in the diary of one Reverend William Bentley notes that Woodman was "in search of manganese in this quarter," a rather clear indication that here, too, black-glazed wares were being manufactured.

Due north of Poultney and not far from Vergennes was the kiln of Caleb Wright at New Haven. Established in 1830 and existing for a decade or two, this shop turned out earthenware with a yellowish glaze. Several examples including jars and milk pans have been identified.

Yet another northern Vermont kiln was at St. Johnsbury, a town better known for its stoneware factory. William and Ebenezer Hutchinson of Lyndeborough made redware here from 1815 until 1840.

It was not surprising that the Hutchinsons had to compete with stoneware. The overwhelming presence of the stoneware factories at Bennington, Burlington, St. Albans, St. Johnsbury, and Fairfax after 1840 made it highly unlikely that any redware manufactory could succeed in Vermont unless it confined itself to flowerpots or roofing tile.

Moreover, all the stoneware kilns also produced redware, particularly in the earlier days. John Norton, founder of the great Bennington shop, is known to have made red earthenware at least until the 1830s, and several examples from his kiln have been identified. In fact, according to the diary of a neighbor, Hiram Harwood, Norton had two kilns, one of which was used exclusively for lead-glazed wares.

Likewise, Jonathan Fenton, a stoneware potter from New Haven, Connecticut, who settled in the vicinity of Dorset in 1801 made redware as well as stoneware. Watkins found numerous red earthen sherds at his kiln sites in Dorset Hollow and East Dorset. He and his sons were active at the latter location until about 1835. Fenton's

brother, Richard Webber, founded the St. Johnsbury works in 1808, and his son, Leander, carried it on until the entire complex burned to the ground in 1859. In the early years, redware pottery was the exclusive output, and even during the 1830s and 1840s a substantial amount of it was produced.

In fact, even the famous United States Pottery Company of Bennington, which from 1847 to 1858 challenged the world's leading manufacturers of porcelain and Rockingham, made redware. Among the rarities produced there is a "sweetheart" pattern pitcher on the base of which is incised "Hoosac Red Clay," reflecting the fact that the material from which it was made originated in the valley of the Hoosic River, a stream that flows near Bennington.

With competition like this, it is hardly surprising that the redware potteries of Vermont were never able to establish themselves as long-term, viable operations.

5

CONNECTICUT, RHODE ISLAND, AND MAINE

THE NEW ENGLAND "border" states of Connecticut and Maine present contrasting but largely successful developments of the potter's craft. The former, closest to stoneware clay that was available at Huntington, New York, a few miles across Long Island Sound, had a substantial stoneware industry from the mid-eighteenth century. But it also supported several traditional redware potting centers, among which was Norwalk, source of the highly collectible slip-decorated pie plates.

Maine, on the other hand, was so far from sources of stoneware clay that its stoneware kilns often languished, while myriad redware potters, both in larger communities and backwoods boroughs, flourished late into the nineteenth century.

Rhode Island, sandwiched between the aggressive and well-established craftsmen of Connecticut and Massachusetts, never developed a significant ceramic industry, but remained a market for wares made in neighboring states.

CONNECTICUT

While Connecticut potters turned out many objects indistinguishable from those made in Massachusetts, New Hampshire, or Vermont, certain of their wares were unique. Pie plates with notched edges, marked either with a knife or with a coggle wheel run around the rim, are found only here. All other New England pie plates have smooth rims. Slip-script decoration, practiced primarily at the Norwalk potteries, is almost synonymous with Connecticut redware, as are egg-shaped preserve jars with domed lids and the myriad bright red vessels splashed with black.

Though the largest kilns were located in major communities like Hartford, Norwich, and Norwalk, some of the earliest were in tiny inland towns. John Pierce worked at Litchfield in the northwestern part of the state from 1752 until his death in 1783, and Philemon Adams was at Pomfret in the northeast corner around

1785. A few miles north of here, at South Woodstock, Thomas Bugbee, Jr., established a redware kiln in 1793 that operated until 1843. Bugbee's trade must have been substantial because he is recorded as having burned six kilns of ware in one summer, amounting to some 5,000 pieces, 40 percent of which were milk pans.

Best-known of these rural shops was the one at Goshen some ten miles northwest of Litchfield. In 1776 Jonathan Kettle, grandson of James Kettle, the well-known Danvers, Massachusetts, craftsman, went into business here. Among his apprentices may have been John Norton of Bennington, Vermont, who was born in the village and lived there until 1785. Kettle was succeeded around 1790 by Jesse Wadhams, and his employee was Hervey Brooks, to whose diligence we owe much of our knowledge about how a small nineteenth-century pottery was run.

Brooks recorded his daily activities, including work as a potter, from 1802 until his death in 1873. During much of that period he operated his own manufactory, which he appears to have built around 1829. In addition to the account books, numerous pieces from Brooks's hand have come down to us. Some are marked H.BROOKS with his metal stamp (which has also been preserved as has his pottery shop, now at Old Sturbridge Village in Massachusetts).

Much of what Hervey Brooks made was either glazed only on the inside or given a coating of clear lead or black manganese. However, he also practiced slip decoration, which he always referred to in his account books as "painting." Though a few pieces have notations in script—the name "Ann" on a creamer made for his granddaughter, the town name "Goshen" on a jar, and even the date "1854" on a chamber pot—Brooks did not see slip script as decorative, as the Norwalk potters did. It was simply informational or an added touch to a gift piece.

Decoration to Hervey Brooks was the complex scalloping and lines inscribed in white slip about the interior of his pie plates and deep dishes. Done apparently with a single quill slip cup, these designs are much closer in inspiration to the eighteenth-century decoration from the Bayley kiln in Massachusetts than they are to the New Jersey–inspired work of the Norwalk decorators. They are also remarkably similar to the decoration on sherds found at the Nathaniel Rochester kiln in East Bloomfield, New York (c. 1812–29).

There were other potters in the interior of the state. Hartford was an early and important center, with John Souter (c. 1790–1805), Seth Goodwin (c. 1795–1818), and Nathaniel Seymour (c. 1790–1825) all active at the turn of the century. However, Souter disappeared, and the families of the other two pioneers soon turned to stoneware production, though continuing to make some earthenware. The only identifiable piece from this period is a bulbous pitcher at the Wadsworth Atheneum attributed to Seymour. It has a massive handle and tiny spout and is light tan splashed with white and dotted with green in the Massachusetts manner.

Along the coast there were redware potters at Norwich and, of course, Norwalk. The former is long on history but short on identifiable ware. In 1771, Christopher Leffingwell and Thomas Williams advertised for "throwers or wheelmen" for their new "earthenware manufactory" in Norwich; and, in *The Norwich Packet and The Weekly Advertiser* for August 15, 1777, they offered:

> To be sold for Cash or Country Produce by the Maker, at his house near Doctor Lathrop's at Norwich; A New Assortment of home made Earthenware consisting of Milk Pans, Chamber Pots, Mugs, etc.

Later advertisements indicated the proprietors were manufacturing cups and saucers, mugs, pans, butter pots, pitchers, jugs, bowls, plates, and platters. Sherds excavated by Watkins indicated that slip decoration in both black and white on a darker ground was practiced here.

The Leffingwell shop was continued by his son-in-law, Charles Lathrop, through 1794, but sometime before that stoneware had become the major product. Two years later the kiln was sold to Christopher Potts and son, who advertised the manufacture of "all kinds" of earthenware, but dissolved their partnership in the next year. The shop may have remained active under other management until around 1812.

From the point of view of the collector, the most important redware potteries in Connecticut were those located in Norwalk, for it was here that the spectacular slip-script pie plates and platters, which are now sold for hundreds or even thousands of dollars apiece, were manufactured.

There were three important kilns here. The first was that of Asa Hoyt and his son, also named Asa, at Old Well, now South Norwalk. The Hoyts were in the area and probably in business during the Revolution, though the first evidence of their activities dates to 1796. By 1819 the kiln had been sold. Excavation of the site by Andrew L. and Kate Barber Winton, whose booklet, *Norwalk Potteries*, remains the definitive work on the area, revealed much unglazed and black-glazed ware but also dark red pieces splashed with black (a style of decoration deemed characteristic of Norwalk, though it is also found in New Jersey and Pennsylvania). Most important, however, were fragments of coggle-edged pie plates that were slip-decorated with knotlike loops, which in some cases had been combed while still wet to create a feathered appearance similar to that seen in English comb ware of the same period. Nearly all these plates are also speckled with green in the manner of eighteenth-century Massachusetts work, and none show the slip-script names and dates so common on later Norwalk plates.

In 1793, Absalom Day leased property near Hoyt's kiln for a pot house that he ran until 1841,

Manganese-daubed dome-top redware preserve jar, Connecticut, c. 1820–50. Though the form was also made elsewhere, these jars are usually traceable to the pottery at Norwalk, Ct.

when he transferred it to his son who sold out in 1849. Day had been born and apparently trained in Chatham, New Jersey, and he is thought to be the originator of the characteristic Norwalk slip-script decoration.

Like many potters, Day had problems with his customers and his help. Among the pieces attributed to him is a plate embellished with a plea to slow payers, "Pony Up The Cash"; and, in the *Norwalk Gazette* for March 10, 1824, he warned others against "harboring or trusting" an absconding apprentice:

ONE CENT REWARD-RUNAWAY from the service of the subscriber on the 7th ult. an indented apprentice to the Potting Business by the name of *Jason Merrills* about 17 years of age. Rather large of his age, stocky built, has a large head, large blue eyes and lightish hair . . . Whoever will return said apprentice shall be entitled to the above reward and no charges . . .

Of course, even the most cursory reading of this notice will make it clear that Day was neither greatly concerned about seeing Merrills again, nor would it have been worthwhile for anyone to bring him back. The purpose of such notices, common in early-nineteenth-century newspapers, was to prevent third parties from attempting to enforce debts incurred by the apprentice against his former master.

Interestingly enough, Merrills did return to Norwalk, for he appears years later in a Civil War era photograph of employees at the Smith Pottery. Another and apparently more diligent apprentice of Absalom Day was John Betts

Gregory, who, while working at his own pottery in Clinton, produced the only positively identified example of New York State slip-script decoration. Gregory also later returned to Norwalk where he ran a small earthenware pottery on Half Mile Island from 1832 until 1840.

The latest and most important of the three major kilns was that established c. 1825 in what is now downtown Norwalk, by Asa A. Smith. Like Merrills and Gregory, Smith had been an apprentice of Absalom Day, and though from the beginning he described his business as a "Stone Ware Factory," he, in fact, also produced a vast quantity of earthenware, including most of the known slip-script plates and platters. As late as 1864, a price list from Smith's Norwalk Pottery offered the following impressive list of redware: baking dishes, chamber pots, jugs, storage pots, covered preserve jars, pudding pans, flat pans "yellow- or red-glazed" (probably the slip-script pie plates), pipkins, mugs, cups, pitchers, washbowls, milk pans, teapots, butter coolers, cake molds, bottles, banks, bedpans, bean pots, flowerpots, and childrens' toy dishes.

Most of the Norwalk slip-script ware seems to have been done by the same hand, and local folklore credits it to a longtime employee of the Smith factory named Chichester, either Henry (c. 1762–1849) or Ward (c. 1835–72).

The Smith factory continued under various family managements until 1888, when it was sold to a group of local merchants who soon turned to wholesaling rather than manufacturing. It is not known when the making of traditional redware was abandoned, but during the

A manganese-daubed redware crock from Connecticut, c. 1850–80. These pieces, whose form mimics the common stoneware crocks of the period, are rather rare.

1870s and 1880s the firm produced quantities of terra-cotta art ware that mimicked classic urn and vase forms.

Norwalk's other redware manufactories are interesting primarily for the unusual nature of their products. Several of these, including Henry Chichester, Jr., and James Quintard (c. 1825–38), E. M. and J. A. Wheeler (c. 1853–65), and Russell & Irwin (c. 1852–55) made doorknobs and drawer pulls of mixed redware clays covered with a clear, brown, or green glaze. These so-called mineral knobs competed successfully with the better-known Rockingham knobs made at Bennington and elsewhere. In 1989 I purchased a box containing dozens of these knobs at an East Norwalk house sale. The owners professed not to know their origin, but they showed signs of having been excavated and were probably part of two caches of such ware unearthed in South Norwalk in 1971 and 1978.

The Quintard firm is also said to have produced a variety of redware suit and coat buttons, examples of which are on display at the Lockwood House Museum, Norwalk, as well as cones in which sugar was formed.

RHODE ISLAND

Apparently due to the abundance of pottery available not only from neighboring states but also by sea from as far south as Pennsylvania, Rhode Island never developed a significant ceramic tradition. At present only four redware potters are known to have worked in the state, and no ware from their kilns has positively been identified.

The state's potting history is brief and early. In 1680 John Wilkins, who had worked in Boston (c. 1670–80), began to operate a kiln at Bristol, where as early as 1686 he was licensed to

Unusual redware poultry waterer in a yellow lead glaze. Connecticut or Massachusetts, c. 1850–80. Redware waterers are rare, especially glazed examples.

run a tavern. Though he was still referred to as "potter" in 1689, it is thought that Wilkins abandoned the trade soon after for more lucrative activities.

Nearly a century later, the brothers Isaac and Samuel Upton of Danvers, Massachusetts, established themselves at East Greenwich, where they remained active from 1771 to 1783. Apparently, they did not meet with any great success, for Isaac moved back to Massachusetts, and Samuel sold the premises and went to New York State.

Another Danvers potter, Joseph Wilson, settled first in Pawtucket (c. 1767–70), then in neighboring Providence, where he worked from 1770 until 1780. Wilson appears to have always been in financial difficulty, and by 1780 he had lost all his property in Rhode Island. It may well have been due to the competition from out-of-state potteries. As early as 1767, Wilson's ad in the *Newport Mercury* for June 22 informed the public that he "can supply them with Earthen Ware at a cheap Rate, made in the best Manner and glazed in the Same Way as Practised in Philadelphia." Apparently, the citizens were not convinced.

MAINE

Considered a part of Massachusetts until admitted as the twenty-third state in 1820, Maine had an important potting tradition, the history of which is ably set down in M. Lelyn Branin's *The Early Potters and Potteries of Maine.* Two characteristics of the state's industry are particularly striking. First, the bulk of its potters were trained in Massachusetts or New Hampshire or schooled by those apprenticed there. Second, despite the state's substantial size, almost all of its potteries were located within forty miles of the coast. The vast hinterland, even today the province of the lumberman and hunter, was too sparsely populated to support a ceramics industry.

There are several references to eighteenth-century potters and potteries, including the shop of John Day at Pownal in Cumberland County, where an unglazed jar incised "May ye 8 1739 JD/ hur Jug price 2S 6d/ Give me to make with your hand and I will fill it if I can" is said to have been made. This piece would qualify as the

Slip-glazed redware miniatures, northeastern, c. 1850–80. Left to right: pitcher, creamer in green on yellow, preserve jar, and crock. The largest piece is 3 inches high. Such pieces were sold as toys or novelties or given away as souvenirs of a visit to the pottery. Today, they are highly prized by collectors.*

So-called acorn-form lead-glazed redware bank, New York or New England, c. 1830–60. Such pieces were often termed "penny banks" or "money jugs" in potters' price lists.

earliest marked example of Maine redware, but little else is known of Day's business.

A great deal more has been discovered about the Dodge Pottery in Portland. Established in 1795 by Benjamin Dodge of Exeter, New Hampshire (origin of an amazing number of Maine craftsmen), it was continued into 1875 by his son, Benjamin Jr. The senior Dodge appears to have made the usual utilitarian wares: his ad in the *Eastern Herald* of May 18, 1795, notes that "he will keep constantly for sale the various sorts of EARTHEN WARE . . . at the lowest prices"; yet he was also a bit of an artist.

One William Goold, a contemporary, described him as having created pieces embellished with such things as a profile of Lafayette and embossed representations of animals. Apparently, not all of the latter were to Goold's liking for he remarked that:

> the legs and tails of animals seem to have been placed without due care. A horse would have the forward legs of a Giraffe and perhaps the tail of a cow. Cats had a severe curl to their tails like the tail of a nervous dog. (M. Lelyn Branin, *The Early Potters and Potteries of Maine* [Middletown, Ct.: Wesleyan University Press, 1978].)

Artistic judgments aside, Dodge appears to have been one of the very few New England redware men to practice applied decoration of the sort found in Pennsylvania, North Carolina, and Virginia.

His son, who entered the business in 1829, developed a rich green glaze that is found on several pieces from his hand that are marked B.DODGE/PORTLAND. The Dodge Pottery was in business for eighty years (not that unusual in a state where the successful kilns seemed to survive for decades) and might have lasted longer were it not that the son, like his father some forty years before, took his own life.

Other kilns founded in the eighteenth century included one in Buxton of another Exeter potter, James Bickford (c. 1793–1844), continued by his son, James Jr., until 1878; the shop of Samuel and Hezekiah Prentiss (c. 1784–97) at Gorham a few miles west of Portland; and that of Benjamin Porter of Danvers, Massachusetts, active as early as 1790 at Pownalborough near Wiscasset and continued by his son Ezra through 1830.

Of equal age was the shop run by John Thomas in Yarmouth (1791–1836). The Yarmouth business was long-lived. It was taken over by Ebenezer Corliss (who had been an apprentice to Thomas) and run by him until his death in 1853. However, in his early years Thomas encountered environmental problems remarkably similar to present-day ones. In 1793, he bought a local clay bed by contract specifying that:

> Thomas shall make and at all times maintain a good and sufficient Board Fence between said bargained premises and the Grantor, and he the said Thomas is not to extend his Clay Pit to within the distance of four & a half feet of the Board Fence to be built aforesaid. (M. Lelyn Branin, *The Early Potters and Potteries of Maine* [Middletown, Ct.: Wesleyan University Press, 1978].)

Clearly, the neighbors didn't want to look at a hole in the ground.

Yarmouth was a pretty lively pottery town. Corliss had had his own business there (c. 1806–35), and Nathaniel Foster (like Thomas, a Massachusetts potter) ran a shop from 1807 until it was inherited in 1853 by his sons, Benjamin and William Henry, who continued the work until 1891. Yet another factory was that of Joel Smith Brooks and his son, John Edward Brooks (c. 1827–88).

During the nineteenth century there were dozens of potters active in Maine. However, certain ones stand out. Among these are the Saffords at Monmouth in Kennebec County. The Exeter potter John Safford II built a kiln here in 1822 that remained active until 1854; while his cousin, John M. Safford, who arrived around 1845, established a business that lasted until 1921, being run in the later years by his son, George L. Safford. A price list from the 1880s shows that even at that late date the Saffords were still turning out traditional redware forms such as flowerpots, milk pans, bean pots, and preserve jars.

An interesting aspect of the Safford kilns is that they produced marked redware (something more often found in Maine than in the other New England states). Known impressions include JOHN SAFFORD/MONMOUTH and JOHN SAFFORD 2D, both attributed to John Safford II and JOHN M. SAFFORD/STEW POT NO.3 attributed to his cousin. The mark SAFFORD & ALLEN/MONMOUTH, ME. reflects an unknown partnership with a third party.

There is another marked piece, this one from Hollis where John Alld was active from 1811 until 1865. He left behind a jug to memorialize the founding of his business, for incised on its base is J.ALLD/1811. One of Alld's apprentices, Thomas Kendrick, ran his own shop in Hollis (c. 1827–77). Both produced lovely tan vessels spotted in brown.

Another important site was Woolrich where John Corliss, an apprentice of the Yarmouth potter Nathaniel Foster, set up a shop at Day's Ferry in 1824. It was operated by his sons Howard and Frederick Corliss until 1892. Well-formed bulbous vessels with two incised lines circling the shoulder and a pale green glaze splashed with brown are characteristic of Woolrich work. However, the pottery also turned out unglazed spittoons and flowerpots that were painted red or green.

The Bodges were another pioneering potting family. John, the father, worked at Fayette, west of Augusta, from 1805 until 1827 when he moved to Wayne where he was active until 1835.

Covered herb jar with polychrome slip decoration, New England or Pennsylvania, c. 1820–50. These small jars were used to store a variety of dry condiments.

His son Moulton remained in Fayette running a family kiln from 1823 through 1850.

Another long-lived shop was that of the Norcross clan at Farmington. Josiah Norcross worked here from 1800 until 1818 being succeeded by his son, Matthias, c. 1818–68, whose son, Matthias Jr., finally shut down the kiln in 1876.

Among the many other Maine potteries worthy of mention are those of William S. Bennett at Bath (c. 1813–47); the brothers, Samuel (c. 1808–21) and Joseph (c. 1821–74) Philbrick at Skowhegan; James Tarbox (c. 1819–74) at Thomaston; and another father-and-son team, Richard (c. 1815–59) and Richard T. (c. 1859–89) Kittson in Bridgton.

The remarkable longevity of so many Maine redware manufactories may be explained in sev-

Drinking vessels. Left to right: *brown-daubed rundlet or swiggler, Massachusetts, c. 1820–70; bottle attributed to Galena, Ill., c. 1855–70; manganese-splotched flask, Connecticut, c. 1830–50, Ex. col. W. Oakley Raymond.*

eral ways. The area was remote, the people provincial and insular. They were not much affected by fashion. However, one must also credit the ingenuity and flexibility of the local craftsmen. They employed every glaze from clear lead to manganese; they made the forms their customers sought, from smoking pipes (George and Harrison Brooks, Orrington, c. 1855–85) to classic urns and vases (Rufus Lamson and Eben Swasey, Portland, c. 1874–81); and they made pots that lasted, as the abundance of existent Maine redware so well attests.

6

NEW YORK AND NEW JERSEY

AS ONE MIGHT EXPECT from their geographical proximity, the potteries of New York and New Jersey have always been closely linked. John DeWilde, who built and operated an earthenware kiln in Burlington, New Jersey, c. 1688–91, was working in Manhattan by 1697; while, a century later, members of the Durell family seem to have been active simultaneously in New York City and Elizabeth, New Jersey. Throughout the nineteenth century, immigrant potters arriving at the port of New York would work briefly in Manhattan or Brooklyn, then find their way west to Elizabeth or Trenton, New Jersey. As a result, redware form and style in the two states have always shown some basic similarities.

On the other hand, both states are linked to New England and, especially, to Connecticut. Absalom Day, who was instrumental in establishing the important Norwalk, Connecticut, redware business, was trained in New Jersey, as were many other Norwalk potters. And Con-

necticut craftsmen regularly traveled west to New York. John Betts Gregory, who was apprenticed to Day, practiced his trade for years in Clinton, New York; while Jacob Fenton, a member of the New Haven potting family, built redware kilns at Burlington and Jamestown, New York.

NEW YORK

The history of New York State redware potting is as lengthy as its practitioners were prolific; yet, for years the state's output was ignored or mistakenly attributed to New England or Pennsylvania. Prior to the 1970 publication of my *Early Potters and Potteries of New York State*, no more than ten such craftsmen were thought to have worked in the state. My research revealed dozens! The city of Albany alone had twenty-one such kilns, the earliest of which, that of John Klock, was in business before 1790.

Such gross oversight is explained in part by strong collector-curator prejudice in favor of the often more colorful products of New England and Pennsylvania kilns and in part by the early establishment in New York of a viable stoneware industry. The latter point is particularly critical.

Deposits of stoneware clay are located at Huntington, New York, and on Staten Island, both within a short distance of New York City, as well as at nearby Bayonne, New Jersey. The abundance of this clay led to the creation of an important stoneware industry, which by 1800 had eclipsed most of the redware shops in the vicinity of New York City. Moreover, transportation of this valuable earth up the Hudson River fueled the fires of stoneware kilns as far north as Albany; and the opening of the Erie Canal in the 1830s allowed inexpensive shipment all the way to the western border at Buffalo. Few New England or Pennsylvania potters suffered such competition from the preferred salt-glazed wares.

Nevertheless, New York State had an important redware industry spanning a remarkable period of time, from the 1650s when Dirck Claesen set up his kiln in the tiny Dutch settlement that is now Manhattan, until 1942 when the Hilfinger Pottery at Fort Edward finally closed its doors.

During this stretch of almost three centuries, literally hundreds of craftsmen made redware in the state. However, since marked or otherwise identifiable examples are scarce, we characteristically know more about the makers (from local histories, census records, newspapers, and business-directory listings) than we do about their wares.

It seems evident, though, that New York potters were conservative, as compared with many of their neighbors. Most of what they produced was either given a clear lead glaze or one tinted to produce a single shade such as green, black, or white. Only one example of the popular slip script associated with Connecticut River kilns is known, and this was made by John Betts Greg-

A twelve-hole candle mold marked c. 1840–55 by Alvin Wilcox of West Bloomfield, N.Y.

ory of Clinton who had, of course, been trained at Norwalk.

Incised decoration is rarely found. The sole eighteenth-century example is a punch bowl by Cornelius Pullis of New York City; however, the largest representation is a group of five bulbous jars with rope-twist handles and scratch decoration, ranging from flowers to birds and names, attributed to David Mandeville who worked c. 1810–40 at Circleville in Orange County.

Identified slip-decorated examples are equally uncommon, though an inkling of what may have existed (and may long ago have been appropriated to neighboring states by antiquarians) is seen in the sherds excavated at the site of the c. 1815–27 Nathaniel Rochester Pottery at East Bloomfield in upstate Monroe County. Archaeologists working there uncovered bowls and dishes with slip-trailed decoration reminiscent of New England, as well as plates covered with a marbleized glaze not unlike that seen on eighteenth-century English wares.

Black- or manganese-glazed pottery was also manufactured. In 1823 the Troy firm of Orcutt & Nichols offered for sale the "black teapots" so familiar to Pennsylvania and New Jersey customers. The business may have been new to the state, but at least one of the proprietors was not new to the trade. Walter Orcutt was from Whately, Massachusetts, where his family had begun to make such ware a few years before.

There are also a few examples of less common glazes. Both the shop of Clarkson Crolius, Jr., in Manhattan (c. 1835–49) and of Nathan C. Bell at Cornwall on the Hudson River (c. 1834–40) have left us marked examples of Albany slip–glazed redware. Since both were stoneware

Redware bottle in an opaque white slip, New York or Pennsylvania, c. 1820–40. This vessel copies the traditional sack-bottle form, which is usually found in green glass.

Lead-glazed pie plate with manganese slip script by John B. Gregory, Clinton, N.Y., 1823. Gregory trained at Norwalk, Ct. This plate is one of the earliest known dated examples of New York State redware.

manufactories, it is not difficult to understand why Albany slip, which was the standard interior finish for salt-glazed wares, was occasionally employed to glaze the red-bodied pottery. Less comprehensible are the sherds of salt-glazed redware excavated from the site of the Caleb Matthews Pottery at Gerry in Chautauqua county (c. 1822–50). Though employed in southern kilns, a salt glaze was rarely utilized on northern redware. But Matthews was a Vermonter who had worked at an Albany stoneware factory; and, perhaps, he couldn't break the salt-glaze habit.

More customary, of course, were the plain lead-glazed bowls, jars, and jugs made at the Morganville kiln in Genesee County (c. 1829–1902) and at the shop of Alvin Wilcox in West Bloomfield (c. 1825–62). Since a substantial quantity of the ware made in both places bore manufacturers' marks and as both locations have undergone excavation, it is possible to judge the nature of their products. Not surprisingly, these are much like what was being produced at the same time in Massachusetts, Pennsylvania, or Maryland.

Redware jug made and marked by Lorenzo Johnson, Erie County, N.Y., c. 1850–60. An opaque white slip decorated with cobalt blue to imitate salt-glazed stoneware. ▶

Further confirmation of the "mainstream" quality of nineteenth-century New York State redware is obtained from two important period documents. The first is a price list published in 1837 by the Athens firm of Clark & Fox. Though predominantly stoneware makers (located in a Hudson River port town), these proprietors turned out a variety of redware including pots, pitchers, jugs, jars, washbowls, cups, cake molds, milk pans, mugs, round and square baking dishes, teapots, bedpans, chamber pots, and a variety of flowerpots.

Four years later, the potter Elija Cornell of Ithaca in central New York described in his personal journal a kiln of ware including many of the above, as well as additional items such as platters, plates, bowls, pudding pans, basins, and inkstands.

Though hard to document today, the impact

Ovoid redware jug, made and marked by Alvin Wilcox, West Bloomfield, N.Y., c. 1840–55. A simple but graceful form popular with collectors.

Straight-sided redware jug covered with white slip, made and marked by Lorenzo Johnson, c. 1860–80. Note how Johnson changed the form of his vessels to correspond to later stoneware shapes.

upon the New York redware industry of the influx of safer and more durable stoneware products was clearly substantial. As in other states, some potters retired from the field or concentrated their efforts on such things as flowerpots and drain tile that were particularly suited to manufacture from the red-burning clays.

At least one, though, had the audacity to create a pseudo-stoneware by covering redware bodies with an opaque white glaze upon which he applied cobalt decoration in the manner of the stoneware decorators. The technique is an old and honorable one not unlike that employed for the delftware made in both Holland and England; but its use to mimic stoneware is extremely uncommon in the United States. However, the potter in question, Lorenzo Johnson (c. 1848–80) of Newstead in Erie County,

spent part of his career in Canada, where white, tin-based glazes were frequently applied to redware.

New York redware makers were of varied ethnic origin. The earliest were from Holland and England. Dirck Claesen, of course, was Dutch, as were John Euwatse who was working in Brooklyn by 1686, the previously mentioned John Klock of Albany, and Philip and John Carner of Greenbush in Rensselaer County (active, c. 1760–1801).

Names from the British Isles abound as well.

The brothers John and Thomas Campbell were active in Manhattan from the 1760s or 1770s until the end of the century; while other craftsmen like Samuel Osborn of Greenport, Long Island (c. 1819–30), and Joseph Shove of Hudson (c. 1790–99) came from the old country via Massachusetts, where both families were well established in the redware field.

Finally, in the second half of the nineteenth century there was a great influx of German potters. Most moved quickly up the Hudson and west into the less developed areas of the state. Still relatively remote, these areas had room for the trade. Buffalo and Erie County were particularly blessed with these ingenious craftsmen, and the finest of them all worked in the tiny settlement of Bergholz, Niagara County. This man, Carl Mehwaldt (c. 1851–87), produced decorative redware objects that compare favorably with the products of the Strassburg, Virginia, and Bucks County, Pennsylvania, kilns that were also, for the most part, manned by Germanic artisans.

As these various national groups flowed back and forth through New York, they established a unity of standards and style that resulted in redware that was ultimately practical but which, perhaps, lacked the strong regional characteristics so notable in the products of Pennsylvania, Virginia, or North Carolina. On the other hand, these men spread the craft. New York potters moved west to fire their kilns throughout the developing territories: James Bailey of Plattsburg (c. 1810–12) and Abraham Yost of Waterloo (c. 1802–10) went to Michigan; James Francisco of Clinton (c. 1829–31) to Cincinnati, Ohio; and Lyman Gleason of Morganville (c. 1829–40) went to Paris, Ontario.

Strangest of all is the story of Heber Chase Kimball of Mendon in Monroe County (c. 1820–33). He married a cousin of Brigham Young, the Mormon prophet, and migrated to Utah, where he rose to high office in the Church of Jesus Christ of the Latter Day Saints. Though his role as a potter in New York State has been almost forgotten, Kimball is venerated as one of the Twelve Apostles of the Mormon Church; and his name recently came to public notice in connection with the notorious "White Salamander" case. Among the forgeries perpetrated by the defendant in that fraud were several "Valley Notes," once legal tender in Utah. Kimball, along with Brigham Young, had signed the authentic notes from which the forgeries were copied.

NEW JERSEY

Like New York, New Jersey suffered from an abundance of riches, at least as far as stoneware clay was concerned. In 1710 Charles Morgan, scion of the famous Morgan family of stoneware manufacturers, purchased five hundred acres of land on Raritan Bay, a mile or so from the present town of South Amboy. On this property lay what came to be known as "Morgan's Bank," a vast bed of fine stoneware clay, which for over a century served the kilns of the northeastern United States.

Presented with such a source of inexpensive local clay, many New Jersey craftsmen soon turned to the production of salt-glazed stoneware. Nevertheless, both before and after the discovery of Morgan's Bank, redware potters worked in New Jersey. M. Lelyn Branin, in his excellent *The Early Makers of Handcrafted Earthenware and Stoneware in Central and Southern New Jersey*, paints a picture of a society in which the local redware maker often existed alongside the growing stoneware factory; and, in some cases, by adaptation to changing economic circumstances, actually survived it.

The earliest known attempt to establish a pottery in New Jersey involved John DeWilde, whom we have mentioned in connection with New York City. DeWilde was hired to build a kiln at Burlington in western New Jersey and

Varicolored slip-script-decorated pie plate, "Why Will You Die," attributed to the potter John B. Gregory of Clinton, N.Y., c. 1808–31. Perhaps this was a conversation piece?

appears to have worked there from 1688 until 1691, when the site was sold for other purposes. While court papers and other existing documents make it clear that the owners of the Burlington pottery hoped to make fine white earthenwares, it appears that nothing but redware was produced.

A seemingly much more successful redware pottery was operated from about 1746 to 1798 at Amwell in what is now Mercer County by members of the Kempell family. Excavation at the presumed site has revealed sherds of jugs, pots, cups, pans, bowls, and the like often slipped in green, white, or black over a black or brown ground.

And, indeed, it appears that slip decoration was more common in New Jersey than in New York. The work of several nineteenth-century craftsmen who employed this technique is well known. George Wolfkiel of River Edge in Bergen County (c. 1830–67) produced elaborate pie plates and platters embellished with names such as "Sally" and "Lafayette," slogans like the gloomy "Hard Times in Jersey," and even a dish decorated with an embossed profile of George Washington. Though unsigned, Wolfkiel's work may be recognized by its highly stylized

Redware teapot, c. 1830–60, attributed to Connecticut and formerly in the Hampstead House, New London.

slip script, particularly the *y* endings that curl up like a pig's tail or bull's-eye.

Less sophisticated slip decoration was practiced at the McCully Pottery in Trenton (c. 1814–68). Marked examples from that kiln are decorated with alternating wavy lines, chains, and a three-cornered motif vaguely resembling the imprint of a bird's foot.

Other slip-decorated New Jersey redware includes pie plates bearing the inscription "Hancock Pottery" (c. 1826–36), which have been attributed to the shop established at South Amboy by the English craftsman John Hancock, and another inscribed "Rahway Pottery," which is thought to have been made at an establishment located in that Union County community, c. 1800–30.

Despite the fact that the state borders the important centers of sgraffito decoration in Bucks and Montgomery counties in Pennsylvania, only a single example of New Jersey sgraffito has been identified. This is a pie plate incised MANUFACTURED BY/PHILIP DURELL/OCTOBER 27TH 1793 and decorated with three stylized flowers against a white ground. Durell's pottery was

located in Elizabeth as early as 1781, and he was still active there in 1793. Since he was apparently trained in Philadelphia, his preference for sgraffito work is understandable. What is surprising is that other Jersey potters did not seem to undertake it.

But of course, here as elsewhere, most men made plain, utilitarian pottery. An advertisement in *The Fredonian* of New Brunswick for October 1, 1812, described the potter Thomas Eastburn as making "all kinds of Earthen Ware, viz. TILE & DRAIN PIPES Also Pots, Jars, Milk-Pans, Cups, Bowls, Dishes, Jugs, Flour Pots, &"; and most marked New Jersey ware is of this nature.

Typical are the products turned out in Greenwich Township, Warren County, by members of the Seigle family (c. 1797–1860). Examples, all in a brownish lead glaze, known to have been made here include a flowerpot saucer (marked J.SEIGLE for Jacob Seigle), a batter jug, and other jugs, miniatures, banks, pitchers, and a shaving mug.

Another source of marked and thus identifiable New Jersey redware was the East Lake

A pair of manganese-glazed flowerpots with attached saucers, Pennsylvania or New Jersey, c. 1860–1900. Flowerpots were made both with and without fixed saucers.

Pottery at Bridgeton (c. 1889–1914). Though established quite late in the century, this kiln turned out pitchers, jars, pots, and pans almost indistinguishable in form from those popular a half-century before. The majority were given a clear lead finish, sometimes with the addition of manganese splotching.

Of course, fully manganese-glazed wares were also manufactured. Best-known by far are the classical teapots produced at Rahway by John Mann, c. 1830–50. Cast in molds modeled after contemporary English examples in silver or white earthenware, these lustrous black vessels were among the few pieces of red earthenware that ever made it to the dining room table. Mann's products are also among the rare marked American examples. Best-known of the other New Jersey black teapot makers is Ephrain G. Mackey of New Brunswick (c. 1811–26).

A few pieces of figural redware (small dogs, toys, and banks) were made in New Jersey, particularly at the East Lake Pottery and at that operated by the Thorn family in Crosswicks (c. 1815–52); however, this branch of the art seems never to have been as popular as it was in Pennsylvania or Virginia.

Most New Jersey potters were native-born, though English and German immigrants played a role; and craftsmen from surrounding states sometimes set up businesses in New Jersey. Among the latter were potters from New York like Charles Schuett of Egg Harbor (c. 1864–83); and from Virginia, Samuel Houseman of Hillsborough Township (c. 1858–60). However, the majority of these migrants came from Pennsylvania. The previously mentioned George Wolfkiel as well as Asher Bailey of Salem (c. 1820–27) and Joseph Raisner of Lambertville (c. 1824–62) were but a few among many.

And there was the usual ethnic mix; a few Dutchmen in the early days, then many English, Scotch, Irish, and German artisans, all combining their talents to create an interesting and varied ceramic history.

7

PENNSYLVANIA

BY EVERY MEASUREMENT one might care to apply—number of active potters, duration of the business, or variety and quality of ware—Pennsylvania must be counted as the most important American redware center. Craftsmen were active here in the seventeenth century and continued well into the twentieth century, producing a remarkable range of ceramics blending English and Germanic influences and highlighted by the sgraffito-decorated pieces that are generally regarded as the redware makers' most important artistic contribution. Also, in no other state did so many manufacturers mark such a high portion of their output, allowing for the identification and attribution of an important body of work.

PHILADELPHIA AND THE EASTERN COUNTIES

The first Pennsylvania potteries were concentrated in the southeastern portion of the state around Philadelphia, where the counties of Bucks, Montgomery, and Chester are synonymous with fine early examples.

There were earthenware makers in Philadelphia before 1700, and by the middle of the following century the city's wares set the standard for quality. Indeed, Jonathan Durell, a Philadelphia-trained potter who had migrated to New York City, announced in *The New York Gazette and the Weekly Mercury* for March 15, 1773, that his wares were "far superior to generality, and equal to the best imported from Philadelphia." His "striped and clouded dishes of divers colours" reflected the style of slip decoration then being practiced in Pennsylvania.

Among the many eighteenth-century Philadelphia redware manufacturers were John Thomson (c. 1780–90), John Curtis (c. 1781–96) whose son, John Jr., carried on their manufacture of slip-decorated redware until 1811, and Andrew Miller, who opened his doors in 1785. His son, Abraham, took over the family business in 1800 and supplemented his father's

Slip-decorated redware pitcher, Pennsylvania, c. 1830–60. Note the simple floral decoration in brown slip.

redware with both stoneware and finer earthenwares.

This was the usual nineteenth-century pattern. Thomas Haig, active c. 1812–31, also made slip ware as well as some remarkable sculptural black teapots and coffeepots; but his offspring, James and Thomas (c. 1831–78), quickly moved into the stoneware and yellow-ware fields. They did, however, leave behind a redware sponge-cake mold marked J. & T. HAIG. Another long-lasting kiln was that of the Spiegel family. The father, Isaac (c. 1837–58), turned out sgraffito- and slip-decorated redware; while his sons, Isaac and John, who continued the business until 1890, preferred Rockingham and yellow ware.

Bucks and Montgomery counties to the north of Philadelphia are identified with the manufacture of sgraffito wares and are, in fact, the chief source of these rare and early examples of the potter's art. Sgraffito decoration was usually applied to display pieces, chiefly plates, platters, sugar and tobacco bowls, and mugs, which were intended more to be admired than used. As a consequence, many have incised names and dates that allow for identification of their makers

(and, sometimes, those for whom they were made).

Among the Bucks County potters known to have produced sgraffito dishes are Joseph Smith of Wrightstown (c. 1763–99), whose marked tea canister, dated 1767, is one of the earliest known examples, and David Spinner (c. 1801–11), whose plates, decorated with brightly colored figures of men, women, horses, deer, and dogs, are considered to be among the finest examples of the type. Spinner also produced one of the truly unique examples of American folk art, a diptych consisting of two large plates or chargers entitled "Deers Chase." The left-hand charger shows a stag pursued by dogs, with the front quarters of a horse just appearing at the right edge of the plate. The other bears the incised and slip-decorated figures of two hunters, a man and a woman, on horseback. When the two pieces are placed together, with the one on the right slightly overlapping the other, the whole composition falls into place, with the horsemen, dogs, and deer creating a panorama of movement across the ceramic landscape. In Europe or Asia at the time, this creation would

Sgraffito- and slip-decorated pie plate made and initialed by George Hubener, Montgomery County, Pa., 1786. Most pieces of this quality are now in museum collections.

Rare sgraffito- and slip-decorated redware oval loaf dish attributed to John Monday, c. 1820–30. Pieces of this quality may bring $30,000 or more.

hardly have been regarded as remarkable, but in rural Pennsylvania it was an achievement.

Both Smith and Spinner employed English for the inscriptions on their sgraffito ware, but the majority of makers used German, which was their native language. In fact, Edwin Atlee Barber, whose book *Tulip Ware of the Pennsylvania-German Potters* remains the definitive work in the field, mistook his first sgraffito plate for a European German example! Even today, confusion exists between pieces made in this country and those being produced at the same time in central Europe.

Among the Germanic potters who worked in Bucks County were Jacob Kintner (c. 1780–1840), Christian Klinker of Bucksville (c. 1773–92) whose sgraffito plates were sometimes incised C.K., and Andrew and Charles Headman. Andrew, the father, began the business in 1805. His pieces, which often featured the traditional Pennsylvania tulip and odd, perky-looking birds, were inscribed A.H. or ANDREW HEADMAN. His son, Charles, who continued the business from 1840 until 1870, also made sgraffito ware, some of it bearing his name or initials.

Montgomery County had an even more impressive list of artists. Among the names known to collectors are George Hubener (c. 1785–98), who marked his wares G.H.; John Leidy (c. 1796–1800) of Franconia Township; Henry Roudebuth (c. 1810–25), whose mark was HR or HENRY ROUDEBUTH in script; and Benjamin Bergey (c. 1830–40). Bergey's sgraffito ware differs from that of his contemporaries; his slip decoration was beaten into the soft clay body, creating the impression of inlay rather than the customary slightly raised designs.

Among the most highly regarded potters in the county was Johannes Neesz (c. 1800–30) of Tyler's Port, who has left behind a substantial number of plates bearing his incised name or initials. Thought to have been an apprentice of David Spinner, whose drawings of animals and humans closely resemble his, Neesz was in-

volved in an incident that indicates the humor and independence so characteristic of the country potter.

Invited to lunch by the local minister, he was kept waiting nearly two hours past the customary noon hour of repast. However, during the course of the meal the dominie ordered a set of sgraffito plates for his home. In due course, they were delivered, and the minister was surprised to find among them an extra one upon which Neesz had inscribed, "I have never been in a place/Where people eat their dinner so late."

In fact, sgraffito plates often served as billboards upon which potters expressed their opinions about women: "Maidens and rose leaves/Pass away like rainy weather"; marriage: "Merry is he who yet is single/Sad is he who is engaged"; their own social status: "I am a bird, of course/Whose bread I eat his song I sing"; and social ills that plagued them (and plague us still): "The star that looks down on the flask/Has destroyed the luck of many."

More than any other ceramic type, the sgraffito plate or platter may be seen as a form not only of folk art but of folklore as well, reflecting in its inscriptions attitudes that were widely held in the communities the potters served.

Neesz's son, who spelled his name John Nase, continued the family business until about 1850. He is best known for his use of a black manganese slip (which produced a striking contrast with the red clay body) rather than the white coating employed by other sgraffito artists.

Other well-known Montgomery County artisans included Samuel Troxell (c. 1823–33) of Upper Hanover Township, who left various marked wares, and Michael Scholl (c. 1810–30), also of Tyler's Port, who was succeeded by his son, Jacob (c. 1830–40). While both Scholls made attractive sgraffito plates, they also turned out fine incised and slip-decorated redware covered jars and sugar bowls. Some of this ware bore on the base an impressed flower, thought to be a cypher or identifying factory mark.

And no discussion of Montgomery County potters would be complete without mention of Jacob Medinger (c. 1900–32) of Schwenksville, one of the last of the old-time craftsmen, and one who met his fate in a way only too common to the trade. Inspired by collectors and dealers, Medinger, who had been throwing flowerpots and utilitarian pieces during the early twentieth century, revived the making of sgraffito wares, until he was burned to death in a kiln explosion in 1932. Medinger's pieces, which have been confused with much earlier sgraffito, are highly collectible.

Chester County, due west of Philadelphia, was home to numerous redware makers, many of whom were British and more than a few of whom were Quakers. Among the latter were the Brosius and Vickers families. Mahlon Brosius of Oxford Township established his kiln in 1828 and managed it until his death in 1863. While his business was a successful one, Brosius was also involved in social issues, particularly the problem of slavery. In *The Potters and Potteries of Chester County, Pennsylvania*, Arthur E. James notes that the "Brosius['s] . . . home was a vital station and his wagons delivering pottery were active parts of the Underground Railway. Not infrequently, Negro women and children were concealed in the hay in the wagons normally used to deliver pots and jugs to country stores."

The Quaker potters were indeed a thorn in the side of the slave owners. Thomas Vickers, Jr. (c. 1796–1822), of East Caln Township and his son, John, of Lionville (c. 1823–60) were both active abolitionists hiding runaway slaves in kilns, woodsheds, and wagons. According to James, one "bounty hunter" seeking runaways exclaimed after yet another fruitless search of John Vickers's premises that "you might as well look for a needle in a hay stack as a nigger among Quakers."

However, their advanced social sensibilities did not prevent the Quakers from being tough businessmen. Mahlon Brosius's son, Daniel, who built a kiln at Kennett Square in 1847 that prospered until 1885, produced everything from ordinary redware jugs, jars, cups, and pipkins to sugar bowls cast in the same forms used to make ironstone china, and lashed his competitors with aggressive advertising like the 1873 notice that he offered "drain tile, made of the best materials and not merely warmed a little, but burned as they should be to withstand the action of water."

John Vickers's prosperous business was carried on after 1860 by his son, Paxson, whose untimely death five years later propelled his mother, Ann, into the leadership role. She not only ran the business until Paxson's son, John V., was able to take over in 1874, but also left behind marked ware including a charming birdhouse with combed-slip decoration signed A.T.V. John continued the shop until 1880.

Unlike the case in Bucks and Montgomery counties, gift pieces in Chester County were not sgraffito plates but elaborately decorated flowerpots (often incised with names and dates) or hand-formed figures of humans and animals. Among identified examples of the former are pieces by members of the Vickers family including one by John dated 1838, which clearly states his abolitionist sympathies: "Is this a Christian World?/Are we a human race?/And can man from his brother's soul/God's Impress dare efface?" Other manufacturers of these elaborate, crimped, footed, and slip-decorated flowerpots included the James family, whose shop was founded in Westtown, perhaps as early as 1728. The first firm evidence of its existence, however, occurs in 1790 when it was being run by Aaron James, who continued it until his death in 1823. His mark, AARON JAMES/1805, appears on a piece in the collection of the Chester County Historical Society. Aaron's son, Aaron, Jr., ran the pottery until 1860.

Another flowerpot specialist was Enos Smedley whose West Chester Pottery opened in 1831 and was continued from 1855 by a partner,

Preserve jars. Left to right: *an example in an unusual orange glaze made and marked by John W. Bell, Waynesboro, Pa., c. 1880–95; a Missouri miniature or custard cup 3 inches high, c. 1870–1900; a jar made and marked by Willoughby Smith, Womelsdorf, Pa., c. 1864–1905; and one from New England, c. 1800–25.*

James Donley, until his death in battle during the Civil War in 1864. Smedley not only made signed slip-decorated flowerpots, but he is also probably responsible for the uncommon redware candle molds impressed E. SMEDLEY & CO.

Among the makers of figural pieces or "toys," as they were often termed, was Milton Hoopes of Downington (c. 1841–64). A rather bizarre figure of a monkey riding an elephant is in the Chester County Historical Society Collection.

Among other Chester County potters of note is Darlington Cope (another Quaker) of New London Township, active c. 1831–55. His specialty was black glaze, which he applied to everything from preserve jars to teapots, many of which bore on their bases the impression D. COPE. His son, Wilmer, revived the business in 1875, running it until 1892 when he reestablished himself in Oxford Township, near the Maryland line, where he and later his son, Phillip, remained in business until 1958.

There had been another earlier kiln in Oxford, this one known as the Mount Jordan Pottery and erected in 1828 by James Grier. His son, John, took control in 1837; after John's death in 1866, his nephew Ralph J. Grier maintained the establishment until 1902, when he was succeeded by his son, Stanley, who continued until 1910. Ralph was another hard-hitter, proclaiming in an 1868 notice in the *Oxford Press* that he sold "EARTHENWARE of all kinds of the very best quality. No poor ware 'cracked up' and foisted upon the public."

Among the many other artisans once active in Chester County one might mention Nathan Pusey of East Caln Township (c. 1796–99) and London Grove Township (c. 1800–12), Levi Coates of Londonderry Township (c. 1809–47), and William Schofield, who fired his traditional one-man kiln in Honey Brook from 1891 until 1927.

CENTRAL AND WESTERN PENNSYLVANIA

As the population increased, potters spread north and west of the Philadelphia area. In Lehigh County near Allentown there was the Powder Valley Pottery established by Charles Ludwig Stahl in 1847 and run by his descendants until 1953. Though better known for its stoneware, this shop was a prolific manufacturer of redware as well, particularly in the early days. Other Lehigh County craftsmen included Henry Albert (c. 1810–20) and Samuel Horn (c. 1820–30), both of whom were located in Allentown Borough.

Carbon County to the northwest has a sketchy ceramic history. Though the only presently known craftsman is George Wagner, who worked in Weissport c. 1890 after spending most of his productive life in Berks County, it is likely that further research will reveal other potters.

Berks County near Reading was home to at least one sgraffito artist, Heinrich Stofflet of Rockland Township (c. 1810–46). A plate made in 1814 bears his name. Among the important pottery sites were Womelsdorf, Dryville, and, of course, Reading Borough. The potter Peter Neuman was established at Womelsdorf, some fifteen miles west of Reading as early as 1792. He was succeeded by Adam Weaber (c. 1835–

40), Jesse Beck (c. 1840–55), and Joseph Feeg (c. 1856–64).

One of Feeg's employees, Willoughby Smith, bought the shop in 1864 and continued it until 1905. Smith's ware, impressed W.SMITH/WOMELSDORF or WILLOUGHBY SMITH/WUMELSDORF (the earlier mark) is among the most available of marked American redware. Nor is this surprising, as the kiln was a most active one. In his *Potters of the Tulpehocken*, Lester Breininger, Jr., quotes a local newspaper as describing the pottery as "one of the busiest industries in town with a capacity of 75,000–100,000 pots per year . . . [which] are sold to Philadelphia, Harrisburg, Lebanon, Pottsville and Lancaster."

Particularly in the late nineteenth century, Smith made mostly flowerpots, but surviving marked wares reflect a greater variety, from fish-shaped food molds to penny banks and lovely pie plates slipped in yellow, brown, and green, sometimes in a crosshatch resembling a tic-tac-toe game pattern.

There were also two important shops at Dryville in Rockland Township. The patriarch John Dry established himself there in 1804; and his sons, Daniel, Lewis, and Nathaniel, continued the business until 1880. Among their wares were whistles and other toys, smoking pipes, and slip-decorated plates, some of which were impressed D or D.DRY. A competitor, Lewis K. Tomlinson (c. 1860–86) of Dryville Church, stamped his pieces LKT.

Reading, as a sizable community, had many potters, the first of whom, Conrad Koch, was active from 1767 until 1789. In 1862 Daniel P. Shenfelder opened a large pottery there for the manufacture of redware and stoneware; it operated until 1903. Though Shenfelder's stoneware is often marked, it appears that it was not customary to stamp the more humble lead-glazed earthenware.

There were kilns in outlying communities as well. Christian Link owned a small pottery at Stonetown in Exeter Township from 1870 until

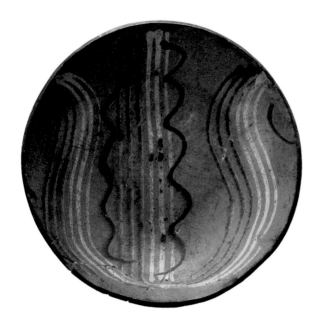

Lead-glazed redware pie plate with varicolored slip decoration, possibly by Daniel Dry, Berks County, Pa., c. 1847–70.

his death in 1909. Some of his wares, which included decorative urns over two feet in diameter, were impressed D.LINK/EXETER/POTTERY. Near Strausstown in Upper Tulpehocken Township was the shop of Joseph S. Henne, active c. 1846–62. Henne's mark, usually struck more than once on a single piece, was J.S.HENNE. It was often accompanied by impressed decoration in the form of birds, flowers, bells, or human figures. In Pennsylvania as elsewhere, such elaboration was unusual.

Other rural kilns included those of John George Buehler (c. 1845–87) at Leesport in Ontelaunee Township; Henry Frey, who ran the first manufactory at Freystown, Washington Township (c. 1810–21); and Mathias Frantz, who owned two potteries near the present-day Bethel in Tulpehocken Township from 1820 until they were passed to his sons, Henry and Isaac, who operated them until 1880 and 1861 respectively.

In Lebanon County, just west of Berks, was the kiln of Henry McQuate at Meyerstown on the present Route 422, east of Lebanon. Active c. 1845–59, McQuate manufactured a variety of redware, including miniatures and pieces with a rich green glaze. Later and less well known was the kiln of William Weidel, a former Berks County craftsman, who ran a business in Jackson Township for some years after 1888.

Lancaster, the county adjoining Chester on the west, was an important potting center, with some two hundred craftsmen working in the area between 1720 and 1931. Perhaps the most important wares were pie plates and flowerpots produced by members of the Bixler family at their Brecknock Township works (c. 1814–47). Though it is not entirely clear, it seems likely that three Bixlers, Abraham (1782–1847) and his sons, Absalom (1820–84), and David (1805–?), worked here, leaving behind several pie plates showing a characteristic wide rim upon which names, dates, and inscriptions were impressed with printer's type and surface decoration of animals and humans done (in some cases with the help of stencils) in slip, incising, and sgraffito. The Bixler work, all of which seems to be at the Henry Francis du Pont Winterthur Museum, is distinctly different from anything else done in Pennsylvania or elsewhere, to my knowledge.

Quite different were the wares turned out in the borough of Lancaster by the Gast, Gantz, and Swope families. Henry Gast, who owned a pottery on Manor Street from 1838 to 1894, also joined his son Henry Jr. in operation of a shop on South Queen Street from 1860, which the latter continued until 1913. Much of what they made, including such exotics as water fountains, figural pieces, umbrella and cane handles, and even crematory urns, was cast in molds; and white earthen bodies, as well as redware bodies, were employed. The mark EAGLE PORCELAIN WORKS/LANCASTER CITY PA/HENRY GAST S Q ST. is found on some of these pieces.

Another Gast, Conrad, whose works on North Prince Street were active from 1841 until 1892, also produced molded wares, including manganese-splashed pitchers impressed C.GAST, which in form closely resemble examples made in Rockingham.

A formidable competitor was Henry W. Gantz whose pottery on East Orange Street turned out redware, some impressed GANTZ/ E.ORANGE ST LANC PA, from 1842 until 1870. His son, also Henry, continued the business until 1880.

The fourth major Lancaster shop was that of Daniel Swope on North Mary Street (c. 1869–92). Included among his wares are examples impressed D.SWOPE & SON/LANCASTER,PA., reflecting the involvement of his son, George W.

Another Swope, Henry, was active at Mechanicsburg in Upper Leacock Township c. 1850–84. Though his shop turned out about 3,500 pieces of redware each year, only a single marked example, an elaborately molded inkstand, is known.

Among other important Lancaster County craftsmen are Samuel Dailey of Elizabethtown (c. 1852–72), whose output included batter jugs, an uncommon form in redware; Jacob Albright (referred to in contemporary records as "the honest tiler"), who made roof tiles in Frysville c. 1786–1800; Joseph Gensemer of Hahnstown in Ephrata Township (c. 1849–81); Abraham Long, a pioneer whose log shop was located in Maytown, East Donegal Township, c. 1779–99; and Tyson Reynolds, active in Fulton Township (c. 1869–85) at a pottery established by his father, Josiah, before 1840.

York County, across the Susquehanna River from Lancaster, could boast of fewer manufactories. Among the more successful owners were Jesiah Shorb (c. 1863–82) of Hanover in West Manheim Township, who turned out some interesting hand-formed animal miniatures; Henry Miller, whose pottery was located, c. 1851–80, on East Market Street in York; and Jesse Kersey, also of York (c. 1790–1824), who made at least one marked piece, a jug incised J.KERSEY, which is at the Chester County Historical Society.

Though far better known for their manufacture of stoneware, the Pfaltzgraff family also produced redware in York. George Pfaltzgraff was active in Conewago Township in 1818, and by 1860 he had a kiln near Emigsville in Manchester Township, where he made utilitarian articles until 1870. The business was continued through the decade by his sons, George B. and John B.

Harrisburg, the state capital, is located in Dauphin County and was the site of several early redware shops. A German potter, Sebastian Snyder, was established here by 1792, and he was active until 1805. Other Snyders continued the business: Peter, c. 1811–17 and Daniel, in partnership with Peter, c. 1834–58. A second important pottery was that of Philip Kline (c. 1817–1840). By 1860 a major stoneware pottery, Cowden & Wilcox, had taken over the local business. However, as pointed out in Jeanette Lasansky's helpful booklet, *Central Pennsylvania Redware Pottery 1780–1904*, this firm also made great quantities of unmarked redware. In 1870 alone, 14,000 gallons, valued at $16,000, were turned out.

There were important sites in outlying areas as well. In Washington Township, Lewis Neiffer established a shop in 1855 that was run into the 1870s by his sons, William and Henry John. Not far away was the pottery owned c. 1860–80 by John K. Enterline and his son, Joseph. Other potters about which little is known include George Etzweiller (c. 1837–49) in Millersburg Township, William Quigly (c. 1799–1805) in Lower Paxton, and Jacob Bacher (c. 1785–1800) and Frederick Gilbert (c. 1800–07), both of whom were located in Lebanon Township, which became Lebanon County in 1813.

Northumberland County just above Dauphin had a substantial number of kilns including one at Milton on the Susquehanna, owned first by Adam Gudenkast (c. 1817–23) and then Jacob Bastian (c. 1823–58). The manufactory was purchased by an employee, William Freed, who

Elaborately slip-decorated oval platter, Pennsylvania, c. 1830–60. Pennsylvania craftsmen specialized in these complex designs.

---

continued it from 1858 until 1882. A decorated pie plate signed in slip script, JACOB/BASTIAN/MILTON/1858 is at the Packwood House Museum. A second Milton firm was started in 1826 by John Leib and continued until 1882 by John Steis. Yet a third local business was that of Francis Shearer (c. 1850–73) and continued into the late 1870s by Isaac Marsh.

In Northumberland, another river town to the south, a pottery started by Jacob Bastian in 1817 (before he moved to Milton) was taken over by Daniel and later Henry Gossler, active c. 1832–70. Also active here (c. 1812–20) was John Leisinring.

The county's first pottery was located in Lower Mahoning Township, where Daniel

Seisholtz established himself in 1798. He was still working in 1811, and other members of the family (Hugh, c. 1839–55, and John and David, c. 1864–70), continued the trade through the nineteenth century. No doubt a sharp competitor was John Leffler, whose nearby shop operated from 1811 until 1835.

Several additional manufactories were located to the north in Montour and Columbia counties. The former was not established until 1850, when redware making was already on the decline, and had only a single shop of any consequence, that of Daniel Ack who went into business at Mooresburg in 1857. Other members of the family, Clyde Edward and John F., continued the business until 1904. They made much stoneware but also redware, such as poultry waterers, flowerpots, stovepipe collars, and even miniatures, one of which, dated "2/16/04," was probably one of the last pieces made before the kiln was fired for the final time.

Columbia County had a much earlier pottery, that of Paul Thompson (c. 1798) at Berwick on the Susquehanna. He was followed by sons Alexander and Hugh, who continued until 1841; and a third generation, in the person of Joseph D. Thompson, went on through 1876. Another enduring family enterprise was that of the Parkers in Greenwood Township. Working from 1826 until after 1876 at two shops near Millville, they turned out everything from jugs, pots, and pie plates to figural match holders such as the one by John H. Parker (c. 1853–76) that featured a bear and a man playing hide-and-seek around a tree stump. Kester Parker, who operated the other family kiln (c. 1854–69), marked some of his redware.

Other local shops were those of John and Elias Hicks (c. 1847–69) in Bloom County, that of Alexander Thompson of Berwick at Espy (c. 1820–32), and a business run in Orange Township from 1841 until about 1849 by Thomas and Ephriam Parker.

Lycoming County potteries were centered around the important community of Williamsport. At Jaysburg was a shop founded by Joseph King in 1800 and continued for some years after 1833 by John King. Slip-decorated pie plates, including one with a representation of Henry Clay, were made here, as well as what John King described in an 1844 edition of the Clinton County Times as redware of "every variety of patterns and qualities."

In Pennsdale there was Job Packer (c. 1820–35) and in Williamsport proper, three larger, later potteries. Two of these, that of William Sloatman and Jacob Ream (c. 1859–83) and George Eakins (c. 1859–61), made only red earthenware. The third manufacturer, William Sipe, turned out redware from 1867 until 1875, but thereafter focused on stoneware, which the Sipe family produced successfully until 1893.

West of Lycoming is Clinton County where Lock Haven, another Susquehanna port, was the major center. A German immigrant, William Shroat, built a pottery here in 1855 on land owned by one Barney Marshall (hence, the term Marshall's Pottery applied to the works). Upon Shroat's death in 1866 another German potter, Bernard Hoffard, bought the equipment with which he manufactured redware until 1884. At Loganton south of the river there were two potters: Joseph Kemmerer (c. 1857–64) and John Gerstung (c. 1870–80). Both made utilitarian redware, and Gerstung made some stoneware as well.

West of the Susquehanna, there were important potteries in Adams, Franklin, Cumberland, and Perry counties. Gettysburg, scene of the Civil War engagement, is in Adams County; and a late-nineteenth-century redware potter, Henry Speece (c. 1885–93) took advantage of the notoriety attached to Seminary Ridge where his kiln was located to do a land-office business in ceramic souvenirs. These included cast plaques of Abraham Lincoln, miniature jugs and canteens, and replicas of battlefield monuments. All were unglazed, and, according to Speece's business card, they were "made from Material taken from the most Historical portions of the Field" so that "they are in themselves relics."

In Bonaughton Township was the shop of David Ditzler (c. 1850–58), known chiefly for the fact that Anthony W. Baecher, the renowned Virginia craftsman, worked here briefly (c. 1849–50) before moving to Maryland and, eventually, to Winchester, Virginia. An elaborate redware watch hutch that Baecher made at Ditzler's pottery is incised ANTHONY BAECHER 1850, JOURNEYMAN POTTER, BORN IN BAVARIA. It is in the collection of the Philadelphia Museum of Art.

There were also some much longer-lived manufactories in Adams County. The Miller Pottery near Hampton in Franklin Township was established by Adam Miller around 1800, and in the late 1820s passed into the hands of his son, John, who continued the works until his death in 1860. In 1863, the business was reestablished just a short distance away at the home of John's son, Solomon, where it remained until the turn of the century. Several signed pieces associated with these potteries are known, most bearing the names of Solomon and his brother, Adam C.

Other Millers were active in the county. Adam worked in Reading Township (c. 1807–28); while John Miller was succeeded by Peter Miller (c. 1814–27) in Hamilton Township.

Gettysburg, as the largest community, had a number of craftsmen, particularly during the period of 1807 to 1814, when no fewer than nine potters were active. However, there appears to have been no shop of significant duration until 1850, when Edward Menchey took over the site on Washington Street and ran it until 1881.

Franklin County, across South Mountain from Adams, can boast of one of the best-known American redware potteries, that of the Bell family. John Bell, trained by his father, Peter, in Winchester, Virginia, opened a pottery at Chambersburg on the "Great Wagon Road" in 1827. In 1833 he moved to Waynesboro, a few miles to the southeast, where he built a factory continued after his death in 1880 by his sons, John W. Bell (1880–95) and Upton Bell (1895–99).

The Bells, particularly John, marked a high percentage of their wares, which ranged from ordinary unglazed flowerpots to extraordinary sculptural figures, such as the massive lions in the collections of the Henry Ford and Henry Francis du Pont Winterthur museums. Moreover, they were seldom satisfied with a clear lead glaze, employing reds, greens, whites, browns, blacks, and even blues in a rainbow of surface decoration.

The Bell factory, which produced much stoneware as well as redware, dominated the

Redware wax-sealer preserve jar made and marked by John Bell, Waynesboro, Pa., c. 1860–80. These canning jars were sealed with a wax-covered tin disk.

earthenware market in south-central Pennsylvania for over half a century; and collectors who may know little else about Pennsylvania wares are familiar with the impression, JOHN BELL/ WAYNESBORO.

Cumberland County, to the north, had numerous kilns. Shippensburg, some thirty-five miles southwest of Harrisburg, was the most important center. In 1817 John Carey built a shop on Penn Street, which he operated with various partners until his death in 1850. His heirs sold to Henry (the Adams County craftsman) and Samuel Speece who were in business until 1873. Down Penn Street was the pottery of Valentine Rudolph, active from 1867 until 1888. Wares made by the Shippensburg firms seem to have been quite varied in form; everything from flowerpots and storage jars to much less common items like candlesticks, mugs, and even Staffordshire-type dogs for the mantel and to be used as doorstops. Most were just lead-glazed, but they were also frequently marked. The impressions J.CAREY, J.CAREY & CO., H.M. SPEECE, and V.RUDOLPH occur frequently in the area.

Two other important sites were in South Middleton Township and at the community of Newville. Joseph S. Keeny opened the former in 1868, and it was operated until 1885 by H. S. Keeny in partnership with Isaac Machett. A New York State potter who had made stoneware at Cornwall on the Hudson from 1850 until 1867, Machett came to Pennsylvania to work for Henry Zigler, who had founded the Newville manufactory in 1852. This pottery was continued through 1875 by the brothers John and Edwin Hays. At least one piece of marked redware remains to commemorate Henry Zigler.

Perry County to the north had only a few successful potteries. Newport on the Juniata River was the most important location. The business here was established in 1838 by George Miller and run by his offspring until 1895. During the later years, stoneware was added to the customary line of lead-glazed earthenware. Other shops of shorter duration were those of George Rupert (c. 1852–61) in New Germantown, William Allen (c. 1840–1861) of Kennedy's Valley, and Peter Updegraff (c. 1829–50) at Warm Springs.

North of the Juniata River are Snyder, Center, and Union counties. Snyder's longest-lasting manufactory was at Beavertown on the present Route 522. Founded in 1817 by Adam Specht, who ran it until 1858, the shop was kept active by Bernard Hoffer through 1861. To the northeast was Penns Creek, where Adam Rheam worked (c. 1826–32), and to the east Mount Pleasant Mills, home to the potter Jacob Arbogast from 1838 until 1876. Other Snyder County craftsmen include Andrew Roush (c. 1823–48) of Freeburg, four miles northeast of Mount Pleasant Mills, and John Price, active off and on in Monroe Township from 1859 until 1878. Interestingly enough, however, the only

documented ware from the entire county are three wonderful sugar bowls with pierce-work decoration, all made and signed in 1858 by Anthony Noll, a potter who worked (presumably for someone else) in Monroe Township.

Mifflinburg on Buffalo Creek in Union County had a long-established pottery. Built in 1796 by Christian Brown, a Berks County craftsman, it was taken over in 1817 by Joseph Kimple, who ran it until 1841. Another shop was established in 1826 by James Eilert, who remained in business until 1868, and yet a third, that of John Wolf, appeared in 1842. An employee, Samuel Getgan, took control in 1849 and went on until 1863.

Another early kiln was that of John Leisinring at Lewisburg on the West Branch of the Susquehanna. Opened in 1796, it was taken over in 1812 by Philip Lester who was gone by 1815. From 1849 until 1855 three members of the Hunter family, Hugh, Robert, and Montgomery, worked in Lewisburg, probably at the same site.

A final location of importance in Union County was New Berlin, where the first pottery was established by Philip Berger in 1799. Adam Maize, who took over from 1804 until 1809, was the scion of a family that ran a shop in Union Township on Penns Creek from 1826 until 1850. The New Berlin kiln was run by various potters, including Philip Seebold (c. 1811–23), Jacob Arbogast (c. 1829–32), and finally Jacob Maize (c. 1861–70), whose death signaled the end of this shop. A second manufactory in New Berlin was that of the Neiman family, operated from 1855 until 1887 by James Neiman.

Centre County southwest of Union contained several important pottery sites. At Hublersburg in the northwest corner, Henry Berry built a kiln in 1830, which was run by another member of the family, Philip, until 1849; it was then sold to John Teats, who continued until 1881. Another Berry family pottery, also in Bald

Eagle Township, had been established in 1814 by Philip Sr. and was run by his sons, Jacob and William, until 1839.

On west Main Street in Millheim there was a redware manufactory established by Abraham Moyer (c. 1806–11) and later run by John and Henry Shenefelt (c. 1811–32), Solomon Fisher (c. 1834–39), John Teats (who later moved to Hublersburg) c. 1837–47, and by John Maize during the periods 1851 to 1866 and 1871 to 1874.

During the time Maize was in residence, some interesting ware was made here including children's rattles in the form of geese and a very large lead-glazed eagle. Oddly enough, the only known marked example is an ordinary, unglazed redware stove collar impressed H.H. WEISER W.S. MAIZE, MILLHEIM.

Other local kilns include one at Woodward founded in 1802 by Ludwig Dornmeyer and occupied successively by over a half-dozen craftsmen, including George Snyder (c. 1836–61), whose ware impressed G.S. still remains. Other important makers were Jesse Adams (c. 1846–49) in Boggs Township, Samuel Wasson (c. 1840–75) in Ferguson Township, John B. Leathers, Jr. (c. 1856–89), at Mount Eagle, and Isaac Lamborn (c. 1803–35) in Patton Township.

Little seems to be presently known about the far western Pennsylvania redware potteries. Though the area was settled later and much of it is rugged and mountainous, there were certainly craftsmen available to supply the needs of settlers. Most so far identified are in the Pittsburg area.

One of the city's earliest shops was that of Thomas Bracken and Thomas R. James established in 1800. James had left the business by 1807, but Bracken went on until 1825. His competitors included James Barr, whose redware factory built in 1815 remained active until 1847, and Jacob Hoensweiler, who also opened his doors in 1815. His shop was still active in 1856.

Barr's works were located in the southern area of Pittsburg, then known as East Birmingham. In 1826 a local commentator remarked that "[t]he Birmingham Pottery is owned by Mr. James Barr, employs 8 hands, and made last year 36 kilns of ware, the exact value of which at wholesale price is 2,980 dollars 80 cents . . ."

In Beaver County to the northwest, Thomas Jackson made earthenware at New Brighton near the Ohio River from 1843 until 1847; and, at a much earlier date (c. 1810–20) the Separatists of the Economy Society at Harmony had manufactured their own ware.

Greene County, located in the very southwestern corner of Pennsylvania, had an early kiln run at Greensboro (c. 1800–10) by Alexander and James Vance. A partner, Alexander Boughner, took over the firm around 1814. He continued to make redware until mid-century, when he converted to stoneware, remaining active until late in the century. It is said that Boughner salt-glazed some of his redware vessels.

Finally, there is an elusive reference to Cambria County northwest of Altoona. John Fisher, a potter trained in Berks County, moved there around 1879 to open a shop whose duration is presently unknown.

8

VIRGINIA, MARYLAND, AND WEST VIRGINIA

THE MIDDLE ATLANTIC STATES of Virginia and Maryland were among the earliest and most important centers of the American ceramics industry. An authoritative study ("The Traditional Pottery Manufacturing Industry in Virginia," by Kurt C. Russ and John M. McDaniel, vol. X, *Proceedings of the Rockbridge, Virginia, Historical Society*) lists some twenty-six redware potters who worked in Virginia during the seventeenth and eighteenth centuries. Though much smaller, Maryland also had a substantial number of such artisans, the majority concentrated around Baltimore where the first known kiln was established in 1763. West Virginia, on the other hand, was isolated from coastal population centers and did not develop an important earthenware industry. Though redware was being made in Morgantown before 1790, a demand sufficient to justify a substantial number of kilns did not arise until the era of stoneware's introduction, and it became the preferred ceramic body.

VIRGINIA

The state of Virginia is unique in the longevity and vitality of its earthenware potteries. Redware makers were active there as early as 1677, when Dennis White of Westmoreland County contracted with Morgan Jones as "partners in the making and selling of earthenware," and as late as the first decade of this century, when the Bell and Eberly potteries in the Valley of Virginia finally shut down their kilns. But more important than the time span is the quality of the work. While late-nineteenth-century redware makers in states such as Maine, Missouri, and Utah were turning out nothing but flowerpots and similar utilitarian wares, Virginia craftsmen were making a variety of decorative pieces embellished with multicolored slips, sprig decoration, incising, and impressed designs.

Most of the earliest manufactories were along the eastern tidewater where Jamestown, Yorktown, and Alexandria were important centers.

In 1688, the Reverend John Clayton advised London's Royal Society that here "I have found Veins of Clay, admirable good to make Pots, Pipes, of the like; and whereof I suppose the Indians make their Pipes and Pots, to boil their meat in, which they make very handsomely, and will endure the Fire better than most Crucibles." (Peter Force, ed., *Tracts and Other Papers . . .* [Washington, D.C.: Peter Smith, 1844].)

Perhaps already, and certainly by 1690, there was a small redware pottery at Jamestown on land owned by Edward Challis, a wealthy businessman who probably employed professional assistants. Excavation of the waster dump associated with this kiln revealed the presence of traditional redware forms: jars, jugs, cream pots, cups, bowls, pipkins, and colanders, most of which were glazed only on the interior.

A much more sophisticated operation was conducted, c. 1720–45, at Yorktown, where an individual, referred to in official reports as "the poor potter," turned out no less than sixteen different redware forms, including such relatively uncommon types as funnels and birdhouses. The land on which the factory stood was owned by William Rogers, but his wealth and various business connections make it unlikely that he was the "poor potter"; more plausibly, Rogers, too, had several employees.

One of the most important aspects of the Yorktown shop was the level of sophistication evident in its products. Redware made here was fired twice, a bisque or biscuit burning to set the body, after which it was glazed and fired a second time. Though common enough in England at the time, this procedure appears to have been virtually unused at early American kilns.

Rogers's earthenware was usually only clearglazed, though platters were often given a coating of opaque white slip and then decorated in swirled or trailed colors—red, green, brown, and black. Along with the examples excavated at the Bayley Pottery in Massachusetts and the products of the North Carolina Moravian kilns,

these must be accounted as among the earliest slip-decorated American redware.

Much less is known about the products of Alexandria's early kilns. However, they appear to have been subject to a strong Pennsylvania influence. Around 1792 Henry Piercy, brother of the Philadelphia potter Christian Piercy, established himself in the city. It is thought that he turned out slip-decorated vessels similar to those being made at the time in his native state.

It should be mentioned in this context that there was substantial interchange throughout the eighteenth and nineteenth centuries among Virginia, Pennsylvania, and Maryland, with potters moving freely between states. A classic example, of course, would be the Bell family whose members worked in all three states.

Inland, up the James River, the city of Richmond became an important site. The first reference to a pottery in Richmond is a notice in the *Virginia Gazetteer or Weekly Advertiser* for March 16, 1782, which heralded the partnership of Gresham Lord and Jonathan Park in an "Earthen-Ware Manufactory" that sold "all kinds of coarse earthenware." Perhaps not the most upscale approach, it is not known how long the business continued. However, by 1811 Richmond had another pottery, this one operated by a father-and-son team, Benjamin and James Du Val. Though initially focused on stoneware, by 1817 the Du Val works was also advertising redware flowerpots and milk pans. Operations appear to have been discontinued around 1820.

As settlements were established in western areas of the state, potters followed their potential market across the Blue Ridge and into the wide Valley of Virginia at the foot of the Appalachians, where they settled in towns along the Great Wagon Road or Valley Pike (now, U.S. Route 11), which ran southwest from Chambersburg, Pennsylvania, all the way to Tennessee.

By the 1830s, local veins of stoneware clays

had been exploited to establish a thriving industry, but many potters continued to make redware or produced both redware and stoneware. In the west-central area, Botecourt and Rockbridge counties had several mid-nineteenth-century shops. In the former, Peter M. ("Potter Pete") Obenshane, later assisted by his cousins William and Peter, made lead-glazed earthenware from 1850 until about 1880. Included were ovoid jars, bowls, and cups, which, like so much southern pottery, look much earlier than they are.

Nearby, the Maryland craftsman Jesse Henkle, in asssociation with Philip Spigle, set up a small manufactory that turned out similar wares that were more elaborately decorated. Identified examples include ones embellished with scratch decoration and combed slip. A semiovoid covered jar of this sort is marked JESSE HENKLE/ BOTE-COURT COUNTY VIRGINIA/1839.

Rockbridge County's earliest known potter was Benjamin Darst, who came from Goochland County where he had been active c. 1780–84. Darst settled in Rockbridge in 1785, remaining active until 1791. A later but longer-lived shop was that of Isaac Lamb (c. 1832–82) who made ovoid churns, jars, jugs, and milk pans, often decorated with incised motifs and patterns in brushed slip.

It was in the northern Shenandoah Valley, not far from the West Virginia line, that Virginia's best-known potteries were established. Both because the wares produced here were frequently marked and because they were often of spectacular form and color, the redware of the Winchester-Strasburg area has attracted national attention. First to focus on the locality were A. H. Rice and John Baer Stoudt whose book, *The Shenandoah Pottery*, remains the authoritative source. Today, it is not unusual for pieces with the proper glaze, decoration, and attribution to bring prices in the thousands.

The magic names are Bell, Baecher, and Eberly. All three families ran kilns that produced

sought-after examples. First in the field was Peter Bell, who came down to Winchester, Virginia, from Hagerstown, Maryland, in 1824. He remained active until 1845, turning out a variety of redware including slip-decorated bowls and training three sons, John, Samuel, and Solomon, in the craft. His mark, P.BELL, is rare.

The eldest son, John, served his apprenticeship at Winchester, where he produced an inkstand that may count as a prototype for much that was later made in the upper valley. Marked J.BELL and dated 1825 (two years before Bell moved to Chambersburg, Pennsylvania), it is covered with an opaque off-white glaze and decorated in pale blue slip. Any European ceramics collector would instantly recognize it for what it is, a passable imitation of Dutch or English delftware.

In fact, much of the decorative ware made in the valley was of this nature: a red clay body fired once and then covered with white slip upon which (after a suitable drying period) blues, greens, and browns were liberally splashed, the whole being finally covered with a clear lead glaze prior to a second firing.

Technically, such ware is known as *majolica* or *faience*; and it has been made in Europe since the sixteenth century. However, American collectors—who are generally reluctant to accept the fact that little we did in the ceramics field prior to the Art Pottery era was really unique—have tended to ignore this fact.

In any case, Samuel, Peter Bell's second son, left Winchester in 1833 for Strasburg, Virginia, only eighteen miles to the southwest. There he bought an earthenware shop earlier run by a man named Beyers, and established another family pottery. The extremely rare mark, S.BELL, is associated with his sole ownership. However, in 1837 his younger brother, Solomon, joined him, gradually taking over the manufacturing end of the business while Samuel focused on sales. The date of Samuel Bell's death is unknown, but Solomon ran the shop until he died in 1882; and

Redware pitcher with an opaque off-white glaze splashed with green and brown, Strasburg area of Virginia, probably the Bell or the Eberly pottery, c. 1880–1900.

Slip-decorated redware vase, Virginia or North Carolina, c. 1850–1900. A rare form with interesting decoration.

it was continued by his sons through 1908. A variety of marks such as SOLOMON BELL/STRASBURG VA., S.BELL & SONS/STRASBURG, and BELL are associated with this lengthy proprietorship.

Despite the magic of the Bell name, it was really Anthony W. Baecher who set the tone in the Shenandoah Valley. Another German potter, trained there and in Pennsylvania and for many years associated with a Maryland pottery, Baecher built his own shop in Winchester in 1868. His rich glazes, applied decorative elements (anything from leaves and flowers to human heads and animal forms), and sophisticated hand molding were copied by the Bells and by the Eberly family, the third branch of the valley triumvirate. Baecher remained in business until 1889. His mark, a variant of BAECHER/WINCHESTER VA., is uncommon, and most pieces are identified by the characteristic sprigged leaves and flowers with which he adorned his pitchers, vases, and hanging wall flower holders.

Jacob Eberly, who opened his pottery in Strasburg in 1880, was not a potter himself (though a son later entered the trade); he hired skilled workmen. His wares reflect a reliance upon the Bells for color and Baecher for applied decoration. Nevertheless, his firm turned out a variety of colorful pieces until it closed in 1906. A number of marks are known, most particularly J.EBERLY & CO. STRASBURG, VA.

Hardest of all to identify are the works of John George Schweinfurt, who worked alone in a small shop that opened around 1850 in New Market, Virginia, to the south of Strasburg. Unlike his competitors, Schweinfurt was content to leave his pieces unglazed or to dip them only in a clear lead bath. Nor did he mark his wares, so all that we can presently identify from his hand are pieces with a family provenance, particularly two remarkable hand-built terra-cotta banks.

There were other potteries in Virginia, many of them as yet unidentified and unresearched; and there is little doubt that the state is one of the most important in terms of early American ceramics. Nowhere else but in Pennsylvania can we find such widespread use of decorative techniques from slip to incised designs, impressed, embossed, and sprigged elements.

MARYLAND

Maryland, too, is a state with a long-standing earthenware tradition. Redware was being made

Redware whippet in pinkish slip, probably a mantelpiece decoration. Made and initialed by Solomon Bell, Winchester, Va., c. 1870–80. Whippets were among the most popular figurines made in the Bell shops.

in Annapolis around 1746, and in Baltimore by 1763. As one would assume, the latter community was for many years an important center. One of the earliest marked examples of American redware is an inkwell owned by the Maryland Historical Society that is incised BALTIMORE/ P.PERINE/1793. Peter Perine was the scion of a family well known in the Baltimore ceramics trade. His son, Mauldine, built their modest business into a corporation that remained active until 1938.

The Parr family, David, Margaret, and James, established another important Baltimore factory, making both redware and stoneware from 1815 until 1855. Other similar manufactories located in the city were James E. Jones &

Company (c. 1834–45) and the Jackson Square Pottery owned by H. S. Taylor (c. 1872–83).

In the far western part of the state, Hagerstown and Thurmont were well known for their earthenwares. Peter Bell worked in the former community from 1805 until he left for Virginia in 1824, and during his stay there were at least two other potteries in the community. At a later date Henry Weise (c. 1865–75) and Martin Happel (c. 1890–1907) turned out utilitarian wares.

The major force in Thurmont was Jacob Lynn, who was in business from 1853 until around 1880. Closely associated with him was Anthony W. Baecher, who left for Virginia in 1868 but did not sever his relationship to Thur-

Large redware vase splashed in green and brown over a cream slip base. Attributed to Jacob Eberly, Strasburg, Va., c. 1880–1906. Though they look more like storage vessels, these pieces were called vases in contemporary pottery price lists.

mont until 1880. Since Lynn was more a businessman than a potter, his operation did not survive Baecher's defection.

At Rock Springs in Cecil County and close to the Pennsylvania border, there was a very late redware pottery. Henry Schofield, a Pennsylvania craftsman, bought a kiln here in 1880 and a decade later built another small shop nearby, which he operated until 1943. Though his output changed over the years from flowerpots, milk pans, and apple-butter jars to decorative terra-cotta wren boxes, penny banks, and candle holders, Schofield maintained a long-standing tradition. He was eighty-two when he fired his last kiln.

Among the other known Maryland redware makers are Jacob Easter of Cumberland (c. 1845–55), Adam Kern of St. Marys City (c. 1880–92), Samuel Crouse active at Taneytown around 1850, and the Grosh family whose business in Bacon Hill dates to c. 1880–90.

WEST VIRGINIA

Morgantown, adjacent to the Pennsylvania border, was the site of the earliest West Virginia redware kiln and, quite possibly, the first pottery to be established west of the Allegheny Mountains. In 1784 Jacob Foulk (probably of French extraction and known in the community as "Master Foulk") set up shop there, continuing until his business burned in 1827. Foulk's tools, including several slip cups, and slip-decorated redware preserve jars very much in the Pennsylvania tradition, have been preserved at the Smithsonian Institution in Washington, D.C.

Foulk was not without competition in Morgantown. By 1800 John Scott was making earthenware there. In 1814 he sold his facilities to one Billingsley who, in turn, transferred the manufactory to John W. Thompson, an apprentice, journeyman, and later associate to Foulk. Thompson had, perhaps, hoped to inherit his master's shop, and when it burned he immediately obtained the only other available. Though he continued for some years to make lead-glazed redware splashed with black, brown, or white, much in the manner of his predecessor, Thompson converted the works to a stoneware factory around 1840, and it was operated in that manner by his sons until the turn of the century.

West Virginia's share of the Shenandoah riches was focused on Shepherdstown, a tiny community on the Potomac River right at the Maryland border. The redware potter William McLuney worked here from 1809 until 1813, followed by the Weise family, whose shop was opened around mid-century and survived until 1880, when William Weise sold out to the Happell clan who continued the craft for a few more years.

Similar kilns in other parts of the state included those of Robert Brown at Wellsburg, Lewis Pierce of South Wheeling, and David Shorts in West Liberty, all in business between 1840 and 1860.

9

REDWARE
OF THE SOUTH

WITH THE EXCEPTION OF North Carolina, home to one of the nation's most important manufactories, the South is generally not thought of as redware "territory." Nevertheless, several states had eighteenth-century kilns, and before 1830 most potters produced earthenware, or both earthenware and stoneware. It was only after mid-century that one sees the proliferation of stoneware kilns that is judged characteristic of the southern states.

Regrettably, little time has been devoted to the research and excavation of the earlier shops (other, of course, than those of the Moravians); for both collectors and scholars have chosen to focus primarily on the area's ash, slip, and salt-glazed stonewares. There can be little doubt, however, that further study will reveal a redware industry of variety and consequence.

NORTH CAROLINA

By far the most important southern redware-making state and among the most significant in

the nation is North Carolina. There were numerous eighteenth-century potteries here, and the trade remained active throughout the 1800s.

Due both to the variety and sophistication of their wares and to John Bivins's book *The Moravian Potters in North Carolina*, most attention has been focused on the Germanic potters who settled at Bethabara, Bethania, and Salem, all of which are now within the boundaries of greater Winston-Salem.

The Moravians were an insular religious group whose potters trained both in Europe and in the Bethlehem, Pennsylvania, area where they had first settled. They combined traditional decorative skills with innovative marketing techniques to dominate pottery production in west-central North Carolina for over a century.

The first Moravian pottery in North Carolina was established in 1751 at Bethabara, the second in 1771 at Salem, a few miles to the southeast. Each survived into the nineteenth century. Both kilns were owned by the religious congregation, and its voluminous records have provided us with detailed histories. In general, though, the stories of the potteries are the stories of their master potters, for the European apprentice system was closely followed here.

The first master at Bethabara was Gottfried Aust (c. 1755–71), followed by Rudolf Christ (c. 1786–89), Johann Krause (c. 1789–1802), and John Buttner (c. 1802–50). Aust also established the shop at Salem where he was active from 1771 until 1788. It was there, in 1773, that he shaped the monumental trade sign (nearly twenty-two inches in diameter) in the form of an incised and slip-decorated charger, which remains the only known piece of North Carolina sgraffito work. It and many other pieces of Moravian redware may be seen at Old Salem, Inc., in Winston-Salem.

Rudolf Christ, too, came to Salem, serving as master there from 1789 until 1821, and he was followed by John Frederic Holland, c. 1821–43. There was also a second pottery in the town. This was set up in 1834 by Henry Schaffner, a disgruntled journeyman (of which there seemed to have been many within that strict and conservative community) and run by him until 1876. It was then taken over by Daniel Krause, who remained in business until around 1903.

Archaeological excavations at the Moravian pottery sites and identification of surviving wares reveal that the range of redware produced here is not only remarkable, but probably greater than at any other site in the country. During Aust's early period at Bethabara the forms made were essentially continental, reflecting the master's Germanic background. However, once installed at Salem, he was exposed to the English tastes of planters settling the rich Piedmont area and he began to experiment not only with forms but with clays, turning out, with the aid of William Ellis (a potter who had been associated with John Bartlam in South Carolina), a passable version of sprig-decorated Queensware, as well as stoneware.

Nevertheless, the traditional massive redware jars and pots (usually glazed only on the interior)

continued to be made, as well as such standard items as jugs, bowls (both handled and basin form), roasting pans, chamber pots, churns, and flowerpots. To these, however, the potters at Salem and Bethabara added an astounding variety of items, some of which are seldom seen elsewhere. Among these are bottles (including the ringed type), rundlets, mugs and porringer cups, tumblers and wineglasses, skillets, covered bowls, washbowls with central holes to be installed as sinks, teapots, tea kettles, sauceboats, a variety of plates and soup bowls, candlesticks and betty lamps, ink sanders, salts, dolls, marbles, bundt molds, preserve pots, sugar bowls, smoking pipes, and even stove tiles.

A particular specialty was small molded bottles in the form of animals and, occasionally, people. Referred to as "toys" in Moravian inventories, these included such diverse forms as bears, fish, various birds, crayfish, dogs, foxes, lions, sheep, squirrels, turtles, and even naturalistic leaves.

Figural bottles, as well as plates and bowls, were often glazed either by dipping or, as with the more elaborate tablewares, by the application of varicolored slips with cup or brush. Early examples by Christ show streaks in green and

Redware Turk's cap food mold in a yellow slip splashed with green and brown, possibly Virginia or North Carolina, c. 1850–80.

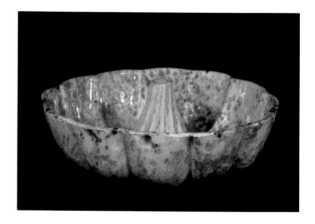

Slip-decorated redware plate, probably North Carolina, c. 1820–50. The wide rim or "marly" distinguishes an eating plate from a pie plate.

brown on an opaque white ground reminiscent of wares excavated at Yorktown, Virginia (c. 1720–45). Later vessels, referred to as "flowered," were decorated with bouquets of naturalistic or abstract blossoms in red, white, green, or brown, over a white or brown slip; or concentric lines, loops, and swags against the natural red or brownish clay body. A few of these pieces bear the marks of masters or apprentices such as John Holland and Henry Schaffner.

Moravian influence was felt not only in Forsyth County where the kilns were located, but also in surrounding areas. Friedrich Rothrock, thought to have been an apprentice, made slip-decorated plates (including one marked FR) near Friedland, south of Salem (c. 1793–1839); while two other men trained at Salem, Samuel Wagemann and Thomas Krause, settled at nearby Waughtown, where the former opened a pottery in 1815. Krause joined him in 1829 and continued the shop until around 1843.

Rowan County, some thirty miles to the south of Winston-Salem, was another important early site. The town of Salisbury had a potter, John Adams, as early as 1755, and Michael Morr worked there c. 1761–71. His son, George, is believed to have continued the business until his

Miniature redware churn with a cream glaze splashed with green. New York or New England, c. 1820–60. Attractively decorated miniatures bring high prices in today's market.

death in 1842. Benedict Mull also had a kiln in this community, c. 1805–15.

Lincoln County to the southwest of Salisbury had numerous redware manufacturers, including John Dietz (c. 1780), who was active both there and in adjoining Catawba County, John Hefner (c. 1790–1800), Jacob Throneburg (c. 1790–1820), Andrew Yont (c. 1814–20), John Pope and his son, William (c. 1819–30), and Daniel Seagle, an early manufacturer of alkaline-glazed stoneware, who, nevertheless, is known to have made a piece of lead-glazed redware initialed DS, c. 1819–30.

Also much influenced by the Salem area potteries was Randolph County, a few miles to the southeast. Philipp Jacob Meyer, trained under Gottfried Aust, is thought to have run a redware shop at Mount Shepard, northwest of Asheboro, c. 1793–99. Other early craftsmen included Peter Dick (c. 1805–10), William Dennis (c. 1810–25), and Henry Wadkins and his son, Joseph (c. 1810–30).

Perhaps, the most important name here is Cole. William Cole was making redware in the county as early as 1792, and his son, Stephen, and grandsons, Mark and Matthew, continued the trade into the 1830s, when most of the family kilns began to produce stoneware, though it is likely that earthenware was still made for several decades thereafter.

Unlike many other areas of the state, Randolph County's redware industry persisted throughout the nineteenth century and even into the twentieth century. William Thomas Fox, a member of a well-known North Carolina potting family, made "dirt dishes" for the Confederacy and was in business c. 1860–90, while other late manufacturers included Hardy Brown (c. 1880–1910) and J. C. Cox (c. 1850–80).

Chatham County, south of Chapel Hill, was home to the potter Thomas Andrews, who was active before 1774. When he died in 1779 his will directed that his kiln and tools be sold. A piece from his hand, incised TH ANDREWS, is at the Mint Museum in Charlotte, North Carolina, along with other examples made in the state. Another important craftsman here was Jacob Fox, from Pennsylvania, who was the progenitor of the North Carolina Fox clan of stoneware makers. He is thought to have produced only redware during the period c. 1800–40.

There were, of course, potteries in other areas of the state. William Goodwin was in business near Charlotte c. 1800–1810, while Francis Stauleer had a shop in Stokes County, north of Winston-Salem, during the period from 1810 to 1820. Neighboring Surrey County could boast of the craftsman Seth Jones (c. 1800–12); while in Almance County near Greensboro, Solomon Loy (c. 1825–40) made both slip-decorated redware and stoneware. His descendants continued to make stoneware well into this century.

SOUTH CAROLINA

Though certainly overshadowed by its sister state to the north, South Carolina had an early and interesting history of earthenware manufacture. The first recorded site is Charlestown and the potter, a Pennsylvanian named Andrew Duche of Philadelphia, advertised his "pot house on the bay" in 1735. Apparently, a bay view is more helpful in real estate than in the ceramics field, for two years later Duche had moved to New Windsor, a trading post near present-day North Augusta. In 1738 he was in Savannah, Georgia, where he stayed until 1743. A piece stamped AD and attributed to him is in the collection of the Museum of Early Southern Decorative Arts at Winston-Salem, North Carolina.

Cainhoy just outside Charlestown was where the English potter John Bartlam set up shop c. 1768–69. Bartlam had come to Charlestown around 1763 to establish a porcelain manufactory based on deposits of kaolin (a chief ingredient of fine china), which had been discovered near Aiken, South Carolina.

Albany slip-glazed redware "face jug," with white pipe clay snake, probably Georgia, c. 1890–1920. These novelty pieces, among the most popular twentieth-century pottery items, are still made in some southern states.

Early redware face jug, probably North or South Carolina, c. 1840–70. Note that the teeth have been formed from fragments of a porcelain dish. These jugs are characteristic of southern ceramic folk art.

The project, however, proved a failure, and Bartlam himself somewhat of a Jonah. Not only was the clay unsuitable, but disease and shipwreck rapidly decimated his employees. The English ceramics manufacturer Josiah Wedgwood (who, like fellow employers, was not eager to see his craftsmen take ship for the New World) almost gleefully reported in *An Address to the Workmen in the Pottery, on the Subject of Entering into the Service of Foreign Manufacturers* (Staffordshire: J. Smith, 1783) that "change of climate and manner of living, accompanied perhaps with a certain disorder of mind . . . carried them off so fast, that recruits could not be raised from England sufficient to supply the places of the dead men."

This appears to be somewhat of an exagger-ation, because by 1771 Bartlam had enlisted a new group of potters and left Cainhoy for Charlestown, where he advertised in the *South Carolina Gazette* of January 31 that he had "opened his Pottery and China Manufactory in Old Church Street." In 1773 he moved to Camden, northwest of Columbia, remaining in business at that location until 1780. Though Bartlam advertised "cream ware" and "Queensware," many believe that what he was primarily producing was slip-decorated redware.

It is possible that Bartlam was succeeded by another English potter, Richard Champion. In any case, Champion is known to have run an earthenware factory there c. 1784–91. None of his products are thought to have survived.

Albany slip-glazed redware jar, probably Georgia, c. 1850–80. Collectors sometimes don't realize that ovoid vessels continued to be made in the South long after they had lost their popularity in the North, so that pieces like this are often thought to be older than they are.

Another early earthenware maker was Adam Effurt, who worked in Pottersville just outside Edgefield, South Carolina, from 1792 until 1830, when he moved to Alabama. The Edgefield district, close to the western border with Georgia, was by this time developing into one of the South's most important stoneware-making areas, and it may have been this competition that drove Effurt from the state. Other eighteenth-century craftsmen about which little is known are Andrew Grenier of Purrysburg Township (c. 1740–50) and John Hershinger of Saxegotha Township (c. 1744–55).

GEORGIA AND FLORIDA

If he was unappreciated in South Carolina, Andrew Duche appears to have been well received in Georgia. When he moved to Savannah in 1738 the city's trustees granted him financial aid toward the establishment of his redware manufactory; and within a short time he had acquired two apprentices, the brothers William and Christopher Shantz. However, in 1743 Duche went to England, and when he returned it was as a merchant rather than as a potter, a trade it appears he never resumed. The craft was carried on in Savannah by Samuel Bowen, whose shop was in business from 1745 until 1760.

Augusta's first-known redware maker was Nathaniel Durkee, maker of utilitarian pottery and tile c. 1801–1804. Though Durkee advertised frequently in local newspapers he does not appear to have made a go of it. He left for Maryland in 1804.

A large number of potters bearing the surname Craven worked in Georgia and North Carolina. Almost all made stoneware; but one, J. R. Craven, is listed as having operated a "factory for making earthenware" in Atlanta c. 1845–50.

At a much later date, S. N. Worthen ran a redware manufactory at Lafayette in the far northwestern corner of the state, close to the Alabama border. He was in business from 1900 until about 1915 and primarily made flowerpots.

Though there is archaeological evidence that Spanish settlers made redware in Florida during the sixteenth century, there is little hint of later activity. The only manufacturer thus far identified is H. F. York of Lake Butler, some forty miles southwest of Jacksonville. York worked c. 1880–90, and the storage jars he made resemble in form stoneware examples then being produced throughout the South.

Handled redware preserve jar, probably Alabama, c. 1870–1900. This unusual form is common in the South but rare elsewhere.

Smith, whose production of earthenware spanned the years 1865–75.

KENTUCKY, TENNESSEE, AND MISSISSIPPI

The border state, Kentucky, was settled by potters from both the Midwest and the South and had a substantial earthenware manufactory. As early as 1796, John Carty and Ward Menelle were partners in a small shop at Lexington. Menelle left the firm two years later, but Carty carried on until 1845, by which time several other craftsmen had entered the local trade.

In time, though, Louisville became the major center. Among the early arrivals were Abraham Dover (c. 1832–48) and George Keizer (c. 1840–45). No less than seventeen different redware manufactories operated in Louisville between 1829 and 1922.

There were potteries in other areas, as well. At Covington, near the Ohio border, Cornwall Kirkpatrick, son of a well-known Ohio potter, worked from 1839 until 1848. John Bauer, scion of a German family that built kilns from New York to Texas, established himself in Paducah, c. 1886–1900; and Adam Cable was active at Hickman near the Missouri state line in 1860. He remained in business for less than a decade, before moving to Tennessee. Little of what these artisans made has been identified.

Tennessee also had a fair number of mid- to late-nineteenth-century redware manufactories. Perhaps the best-known maker of "dirt pottery" (as it was often called in the South) is William Wolfe of Blountville in the northeastern corner

ALABAMA

The state of Alabama lacked early kilns, though it is known that M. D. Preston was turning out red earthenware utensils in Autauga County outside Montgomery during the period from 1820 to 1836. At a later date an important center was the tiny town of Rock Mills, close to the Georgia border. During the 1850s and 1860s there were several kilns in the vicinity. William Mayfield was listed in the 1860 Federal Census as having manufactured some 36,000 gallons of earthenware products, and his competitor, Edward T. Belcher, a Virginia craftsman, could boast of 15,000 gallons, though part of this was stoneware. A William McPherson listed in the same census was probably Mayfield's partner. The business at Rock Mills continued until the end of the century. E. M. Yates was still making redware and stoneware there in the 1880s. At Vernon, on the opposite side of the state, close to the Mississippi line, was the pottery of B. L.

Redware paperweight, Ohio or Kentucky, c. 1860–80. Such pieces were copied from earlier English examples. Here the base is covered with brown Albany slip, which has also been splashed on the figure.

of the state, up against the Virginia line. Wolfe made slip-decorated redware from 1848 until 1878. Adam Cable, who had migrated south from Kentucky, ran a small shop at the hamlet of Sulphur Fork from 1869 until 1875; while William Grindstaff made what he described as "crockeryware such as crocks, jugs, jars, flower pots and tile" at Happy Valley during the period from 1865 to 1888. Examples of his work, impressed W.GRINDSTAFF, are known.

Mississippi was served primarily by Joseph Mayer and his offspring. Mayer established an earthenware factory in Biloxi around 1856, and his family operated it after his death until about 1900. There were also several shops at Holly Springs near the Tennessee border, southeast of Memphis.

10

MIDWESTERN REDWARE

WEST OF PENNSYLVANIA the number of known redware potteries decreases sharply. In part, this reflects the fact that research on this area's ceramics history has tended to focus on the later manufactories, which produced the yellow ware, Rockingham, and white earthenwares for which it is renowned. However, there are other factors to be considered. While there were settlements in Ohio and Missouri well before 1800, much of the region's growth took place during the mid-nineteenth century, a time when earthenware was in decline. Moreover, stoneware clays are abundant throughout most of the Midwest, encouraging craftsmen to concentrate on this medium.

Two other things should also be considered. First, midwestern redware is almost never marked, making it extremely difficult to identify specific items or to link them to a particular kiln site (few of which have yet to be excavated). Second, with the exception of the often spectacular wares from the Galena, Illinois–

Belmont, Wisconsin, complex, pottery from the central states is rarely decorated. A clear lead glaze is usually the most that one can hope for. Given these circumstances, it is hardly surprising that local collectors, as well as most scholars, have directed their attention toward stoneware and the commercially produced earthenwares such as ironstone and Rockingham.

OHIO

Potters from Pennsylvania, Kentucky, and New York moved into Ohio before 1800. Many settled in East Liverpool on the Ohio River, where the vast clay banks provided a source of supply for an industry that is still active. John Koantz, of German extraction like many of the midwestern artisans, built a small redware kiln here in 1817, continuing for about ten years and being followed by Joseph Wells (c. 1826–56). However, by the 1840s the focus had shifted to yellow ware and to mass production. There was no longer a place for the maker of simple redware. Other potters who arrived in the first quarter of the nineteenth century included Philip Brown and Oliver Griffith, both of whom made jugs, crocks, and jars at new Lisbon, Ohio, and Thomas Fisher who turned out slip-decorated redware as well as the usual lead-glazed pieces. He worked at Steubenville in Jefferson County c. 1807–20.

Another early Ohio artisan was Andrew Kirkpatrick, who was trained in Pennsylvania and migrated to Urbana west of Columbus before 1820. He appears to have done well, for the industrial schedules to the 1820 U.S. Census describe him as having produced in the prior year $1,800 worth of "all kinds of pottery ware." Kirkpatrick continued in Urbana until at least 1837. His sons, Cornwall and Wallace, trained there and later founded the important stoneware factory at Anna, Illinois.

Also among the pioneer potters was Solomon Purdy, who made both redware and stoneware for the religious Separatists' Society at Zoar dur-

Lead-glazed preserve jar, Ohio, c. 1850–70, with white slip decoration. Slip used to glaze the interior of this piece spilled down the sides, creating an accidental and almost Oriental decoration. ▶

ing the 1830s and 1840s, after having worked on his own in Putnam County since at least 1820. Interestingly, among the products Purdy turned out at Zoar was decorated redware roofing tile, something that was common in the eighteenth century but at this time seldom made outside Pennsylvania.

While there were, no doubt, many small-town potters in Ohio, craftsmen were frequently attracted to the larger growing communities. William McFarland, a Kentucky craftsman, settled in Cincinnati around 1799, and by the time of the 1820 census the growing community could boast of three earthenware kilns that employed fourteen men. James F. Francisco, who had worked in central New York, opened a shop there in 1831, continuing until 1837; and at a later period Peter Lessel and his sons made flowerpots and terra-cotta wares from 1848 to 1879.

Zanesville, soon to become an important stoneware manufacturing center, had an early redware maker, Samuel Sullivan, formerly of Philadelphia, who arrived in 1806 and remained active for about a decade. Another early craftsman in the vicinity was Joseph Rosier, who settled at Jonathan Creek on the southern edge of the city in 1814. He was followed there at about 1828 by A. Ensminger, whose slip-decorated redware was gradually supplemented by stoneware. In Columbus there was Amos Jenkins and sons, whose business lasted from 1840 until 1868; at Dayton, George Bisch (c. 1858–68); and in Cleveland, Constantine Koch, active c. 1857–68.

Perhaps the oddest use to which the Ohio redware clay was put was the manufacture of coffins. In the 1880s, the firm of Allen & Son

Molded and hand-finished lion doorstop, redware with remnants of original white paint from Ohio, c. 1850–80.

they relocated to the nearby community of Hartford City some fifteen miles north of Muncie.

Michael left the business in 1860, but William continued it until 1878, though during the last eight years activity was confined to the production of drain tile. Only three pieces bearing Michael Cline's mark, the initials M.C., are known; and his son is represented by a single example, a toothpick holder incised w w c 1903 and made long after he had ceased active potting.

ILLINOIS AND WISCONSIN

Though there were more early redware potters in Ohio, the states of Illinois and Wisconsin lay claim to the most attractive and best-known of midwestern wares. The center was Galena, a tiny town above the Mississippi River in the farthest northwestern corner of Illinois, just below the Wisconsin border. Potters from the East arrived here around 1840 to establish a trade

at Mount Sterling, southwest of Columbus, advertised these as being superior to wooden ones since they would neither rot nor allow the entrance of "noxious pests."

Lead-glazed redware toothpick holder, Hartford City, Blackford County, Indiana, 1903. Incised **w w c** *1903. One of Indiana's few redware potters, William Cline worked steadily from 1847 until 1870 and sporadically thereafter until his death in 1923.*

INDIANA

While redware is believed to have been made in Vigo County near Terre Haute, Indiana, as early as 1800 and was still being turned out in the 1860s and 1870s by potters such as Lawrence Schmehr of Ripley County, only a single family, the Clines, is known for its marked and identifiable wares.

Michael Cline, a Muskingham County, Ohio, potter, moved to Blackford County, Indiana, in 1834 and built a small kiln on his farm where he made ware until 1847. That year his son, William, joined him in the business, and

that continued to be viable until 1900. Best-known are Alfred M. Sackett and John Wagden (c. 1858–69), but several other shops were active in Galena, as well as at Elizabeth, Illinois, about thirteen miles to the southeast, and Apple River, eleven miles northeast.

The ware produced in these shops varied in purpose but was remarkably similar in form and decoration; so much so, in fact, that since none of it was marked, it is often impossible to tell a Galena piece from one made at Elizabeth or Apple River. Heavily molded lips and jar rims, semiovoid bodies, and high, arching handles on jugs and pitchers distinguish wares splashed in yellow, brown, red, orange, and green beneath

Albany slip-glazed bank in the form of a spaniel. Made and signed by William Hinzel, Rochester, N.Y., 1901. Hinzel, like many turn-of-the-century craftsmen, worked in a sewer pipe factory. In his spare time, he used the coarse clay to make redware pieces for himself or as gifts.

a glaze so thick that one suspects lead must have cost very little in Galena.

Their remoteness from the central Illinois stoneware manufacturing centers may have spurred development of these kilns, for they seem to have produced a variety of wares remarkable for the time and place: churns, jugs, jars, crocks, pitchers, bottles, milk pans, colanders, spittoons, various miniatures, and flowerpots, as well as unglazed stove collars, chimney pots, and jardineres. There were even mold-formed Staffordshire-type dogs, which served as mantel ornaments, doorstops, or even string holders.

Decoration usually was confined to the glaze, which echoed in its abstract patterns the finish found on certain New England pieces. Coggle wheels were sometimes employed to create decorative banding, the most unusual of which is a series of loops beneath a single line: a simplified version of the Federal swag and tassel pattern employed in the East and South during the early nineteenth century.

In 1842 John Hammett, who had worked at Galena, brought its style and decoration to Belmont, Wisconsin, about twenty miles to the north. Examples of Hammett's work preserved at the Wisconsin State Historical Society in Madison are glazed in the yellows, greens, and oranges of Galena; but the form, particularly the stylish neck and handle finish, is superior, not only to Illinois work but also to nearly everything else done in this country. Hammett must be regarded as one of the outstanding nineteenth-century potters. He and his brother operated the Belmont pottery until 1879. Galena-type ware was also made at nearby Mineral Point.

Lead-glazed redware preserve jar, impressed on base MC and made by Michael Cline at Hartford City, Indiana, c. 1847–60. In 1860 Cline abandoned potting to practice law. ▶

Whitewater and Milwaukee were two other important Wisconsin centers. The former, a small community about forty miles southwest of Milwaukee, gained in 1845 its first potter, George Cole. In 1847 Cole entered into partnership with George Williams, who may well be the man who made stoneware at Athens and Mount Morris, New York, (which would explain why Cole's redware assumes stoneware forms and is decorated with cobalt, which turns purple-black on the red clay body). The firm continued until 1855, when it was replaced by J. C. Williams & Co. (c. 1855–59), and then by Dan Cole & Co., active through 1871. It is evident that these later owners were relatives of the original proprietors.

A second redware shop in Whitewater was operated by two German potters, Michael Ohnhaus and John Milz, between 1859 and 1881. A small collection of Whitewater pottery may be seen at the Wisconsin State Historical Society.

Among Milwaukee's many German immigrants was a group of redware potters who, during the second half of the nineteenth century, made the city the state's most important source of utilitarian pottery and flowerpots. Frederick and Albert Hermann, members of a family that established kilns throughout the Midwest, South, and Southwest, were active here from 1857 until 1898. Busy competitors included John G. Bauer (c. 1857–1905), Frank Mohr (c. 1856–66), John G. Heinze (c. 1867–94), and Wentzel Weitzner (c. 1856–96).

Kilns in smaller communities included those of William Murrey (c. 1865–75) at Brodhead, west of Whitewater; the Batchelder Pottery (c. 1850–80) at Menasha, near Oshkosh; and the

long-lived (c. 1860–88) shop of Konrad Langenberg at Franklin, near Milwaukee.

MICHIGAN AND MINNESOTA

Even the more northern states, which generally lacked proper stoneware clay, imported the necessary means to make stoneware; as a result, there appears to have been relatively few earthenware kilns in this area. Yet, potters skilled in the trade certainly found their way west. Soon after 1810 Abraham Yost of Waterloo in Seneca County, New York, moved to Michigan to be followed in 1835 by another local craftsman, James Thorn.

It is not known where Yost and Thorn settled, but a third New York redware maker, Charles Gleason of Morganville, established a pottery at Burlington, south of Battle Creek, Michigan, around 1865. He was no doubt in

Redware preserve jar decorated with incised and cobalt-filled bird, New York, c. 1820–40. Since it turned greenish black on a redware ground, cobalt blue was seldom employed in redware decoration.

Manganese-splotched redware jug, Norwalk, Ct., c. 1860–80. Straight-sided jugs like this were later and few in number. They are seldom seen today.

competition with Aaron Norris, whose pottery and tile works just east of Battle Creek flourished from 1862 until 1894. At about the same time, there were two earthenware makers in Detroit, Theodore Blasley (c. 1865–75) and Martin Autretsch (c. 1863–69).

At Corunna, west of Flint, Michigan, John Neuffer was active for some years after 1863; and at Ionia, east of Grand Rapids, the firm of Sage and Dethrick manufactured both simple redware utensils and flowerpots from 1893 until 1903. Other potters believed to have made some earthenware were David Striven and Samuel Davis of Grand Rapids (c. 1859–67), Mortimer Price of Hadley (c. 1863–64) and Elijah Nichols of Hanover (c. 1862–65). Apparently, no identified ware has survived.

In Minnesota, the major earthenware centers were Minneapolis and Red Wing. Louis Kampff built a small shop in the former city in 1857. Before 1860, his manufactory consisted of nothing more than a log shack, kiln, and nearby clay pit. A stone building was later constructed and the business continued until 1876, when the proprietor sold his holdings to Jonas G. Swahn, who, with his sons, made flowerpots and terracotta until 1904. There was at least one other pottery in the city, run from the 1870s into the early 1890s by John C. Malchow, who was succeeded by Julius Gobeaux (c. 1895–1901).

Red Wing, on the Mississippi southeast of Minneapolis, was, from the late 1870s well into the present century, one of America's most important stoneware-producing centers. However, there were redware makers here, too. The first was Joseph Pohl, who went into business around 1860, producing lead-glazed crocks, jars, and baking dishes in a turf-roofed outbuilding on his farm north of town. Pohl may have been a country potter, but he was sophisticated enough to cast Turk's cap–type cake molds, one of which survives in the collection of the local Goodhue Historical Society.

It is not known how long Joseph Pohl con-

Miniature footed ring flask with notch-carved decoration, New York, c. 1860–80. This is an extremely rare example.

tinued his business, but it probably came to an end around 1868, when William M. Philleo and Philander Sprague began to make flowerpots and unglazed terra-cotta wares in the same community. Philleo and Sprague were not particularly lucky. Their shop burned in 1870, and though they rebuilt it, they abandoned the trade soon after. An employee, David Hallem, continued on his own until 1877 when he was bought out by the newly established Red Wing Stoneware Company.

Other lesser-known Minnesota redware makers include Charles C. Cornell, active at Owatonna, some forty miles south of Minneapolis, from 1863 until 1871; and Charles Rees, who ran a small pottery at Elmwood from the late 1860s into the 1870s.

MISSOURI, IOWA, KANSAS, AND NEBRASKA

The westernmost midlands bastion of traditional redware potting was Missouri, where the craft was introduced along the Mississippi River by early French settlers. Little trace of these eighteenth-century kilns can be found, but soon after 1800 Anglo-Saxon potters found their way to the thriving river ports. The first center was St. Louis, where George W. Ferguson and Christian Smith were making ware before 1820. They were followed in the next decade by John Taylor and John Bradbury, who were active c. 1820–30.

After 1840, the discovery of local stoneware-clay deposits led to the gradual abandonment of redware manufacture, and only a few artisans, principally located in the eastern part of the state,

continued to pursue this branch of the craft. Best-known of these are the Germanic potters of St. Charles and Hermann. In the former, located on the Missouri River just to the northwest of St. Louis, Joseph Oser's kiln produced household ware in basic forms from 1847 until 1906. While coloring agents were occasionally added to the finish, typical St. Charles redware bears only a clear lead glaze highlighting the orange-red body color. Forms, though somewhat "squatter" than those seen in New England and Pennsylvania, are not greatly different from those being produced at the same time in eastern shops. Ware was seldom marked. A rare exception is a jar impressed F. WOOLFORD/FARMINGTON, MO., which was made c. 1840–50 in the community some forty miles south of St. Louis.

The first potter to work at Hermann, midway between St. Louis and Jefferson City, was George M. Sohns, active between 1846 and 1867. Lead-glazed wares attributed to him include such traditional items as milk pans, nappies, preserve jars, pitchers, jugs, and pie plates. Sohns was followed in the late 1880s and 1890s by a potter named Hoefer, whose output, reflecting changing tastes in the area, was primarily flowerpots.

Iowa had many potteries scattered throughout the state, but they either made stoneware, or their output remains uncertain. Among possible sites are Boonesborough, Eldora, and Ottumwa. However, there is no doubt that redware was manufactured at Sergeant Bluff, just south of Sioux City. The first kiln was built in the 1850s by a man named Wortman. He was succeeded by Charles W. Borders. Known as "Uncle Charlie," Borders conducted an active business from 1870 until 1889 when he sold out to J. L. Mattocks, who was still in business as late as 1895.

Mabel Holmon Gray of Sergeant Bluff recalled in 1939 that:

The products of the pottery were mostly dark brown with a high glaze, altho a seemingly endless number of flower pots of all sizes and shapes were left in the natural sandy pinkish color. The glaze was given by slip. I remember the large vats of slip in which the hand-turned hand dipped pieces went. The slip was I believe shipped in. Sometimes a light grayish slip was used, as for milk crocks. Some times the lower half of the jug or crock would be dark and the upper half light. (Private family records of the Swinney family [Rochester, New York].)

There is no doubt that this was a substantial manufactory. In the 1880s, the *Sioux City Journal* described it as turning out 3,000 gallons per week of churns, butter pots, preserve jars, jugs, pitchers, spittoons, and milk crocks.

West of Missouri the number of earthenware pottery shops is minimal. Kansas had only a few communities where the familiar red earthenware was made. The largest works was at Lawrence, where Anton Grutz had introduced the craft

Manganese-glazed redware: left, a bulbous jug, c. 1800–1830 from New Jersey or Pennsylvania; right, a cuspidor, c. 1870–1910 from New York or New England.

soon after 1865. He continued into the 1880s and was succeeded by the much larger Schilling Pottery, which at one time employed some sixty people in the manufacture of redware, decorative terra-cotta, and flowerpots. This firm, located on what was then New Jersey Avenue, had, by 1890, an extensive trade throughout Kansas and adjoining states.

In Leavenworth to the northeast was the firm of Julius Keller & Company, which made drain tile and utilitarian wares (c. 1860–70). Little is known of John Singer, apparently an unsuccessful rival in the early 1860s.

In Nebraska, where surface clays are common, earthen flowerpots were manufactured in large numbers either as a principal business or as an adjunct to the main output of stoneware plants. William and O. V. Eaton's Lincoln Pottery Works, which operated in the city of Lincoln from 1880 until 1903, kept twenty-five employees occupied in the 1890s and often produced a million molded, unglazed flowerpots per year.

Another kiln, the Nebraska City Pottery, located in the community of the same name some thirty miles south of Omaha, advertised that its red earthenware "would put to shame some of the Eastern potteries." There may be some doubt as to this statement, since the firm seems to have been active only during the late 1860s.

11

WESTERN REDWARE

FOR A VARIETY OF very good reasons, there were few traditional redware potters in the Southwest and West. Early settlers were too few to support the craft and, where available, they generally utilized the native American or Spanish-American ceramics commonly found in the area. As larger population centers developed, those on or near the coast were supplied by the sailing ships that carried factory-made porcelain, earthenwares, and stoneware along the Gulf Coast and around the Horn to California. By the 1860s the transcontinental railroad system was bringing similar items to inland areas.

Moreover, by this time redware manufacture was already in decline throughout the United States. The potters who did move west into the newly opened lands customarily made stoneware. Redware, where produced, was usually confined to flowerpots and architectural terracotta. The exception was Utah. There, due to friction with the United States government and surrounding territories, industrial ceramics were

seldom available. As a result there grew up the most important traditional redware manufactory west of the Mississippi.

ARKANSAS AND TEXAS

Arkansas, especially the counties of Dallas and Saline, produced substantial quantities of common pottery in the second half of the nineteenth century. An increasing population demanded the ware, and geographical factors limited importation. Most of the potters came from Missouri, Texas, or the southern states, and what they made was primarily stoneware.

However, there were a few who utilized brick clays. At Cane Hill in Washington County near the northwestern corner of the state, William S. Crawley built a traditional southern groundhog kiln in 1846 and utilized native soil to make preserve jars, cream pots, jugs, and other useful objects, until he was driven out of business by the "great drought" of 1874. During the 1860s there was a second earthenware shop at Cane Hill, this one owned by H. T. Caldwell & Company. Little is known of its output other than the fact that, like Crawley's ware, it was salt-glazed. The technique was frequently employed in the South, where lead for glazing was often hard to come by, but rare in other parts of the country.

The earliest known Texas craftsman was J. R. Tanner of Marshall, a community close to Shreveport and the Louisiana border. Tanner was in business by 1835 and continued his activities for over a decade. His production, initially redware, was later augmented by stoneware that was ash-glazed in the southern manner.

Tanner was truly a pioneer, for Texas in the 1830s was a far from secure place. Even after the Republic was declared in 1836, migration was inhibited by threats from Mexico and from disaffected native Americans. In fact, it was not until statehood in 1845 that sufficient stability was achieved to allow for the orderly development of traditional skills.

One of the first potters to take advantage of increased order and security was Abraham Babcock, a New Jersey craftsman from Princeton. In June 1852, he bought four hundred acres of land along the Mustang River in Jackson County, southwest of Houston. Superficial excavation of the site has revealed that he made both salt-glazed redware and stoneware here. It is not known how long Babcock continued in business, but he was listed as a potter in the 1860 census of Jackson County.

As the population swelled and trade boomed during the 1870s and 1880s, more potters entered the state. Almost all made stoneware, but a few continued to produce earthenware, either as a sideline or as a primary product. William Meyer and Sons of Atacosa County, just south of San Antonio, turned out a line of redware flowerpots and other objects from 1887 until the

1940s. Other turn-of-the-century manufacturers included the shop of R. Melcher at Weatherford in Parker County (c. 1905–10), a maker of unglazed flowerpots, and several producers of red-clay storage vessels and agricultural wares at Elmendorf in Bexar County.

COLORADO, MONTANA, AND UTAH

The western mountain states had few redware potteries, a fact due more to a lack of population than the absence of suitable raw materials. There were, however, several clay-working centers, one of them at Golden, Colorado, just west of Denver. During the 1870s, Henry Bell operated his Golden City Pottery and Firebrick Works at the corner of what was then Washington and Water streets. The same vein of clay that supplied his manufactory later served the American Clay Works and Supply Company of Denver, which was opened in 1893 by the Montague family. The latter plant always produced red earthen flowerpots, first hand-turned and later mechanically cast.

The only known early Montana kiln was that of Jack Busack located in the Deer Lodge area, southwest of Butte, which was in business from 1871 until sometime after 1875. The *Helena World Herald* for December 11, 1873 noted that:

The pottery and redware works of Jack Busack, near the summit on the Mullin Pass, are being worked with good success. Mr. B. thoroughly understands all branches of the business, and experience has taught him how to manipulate the various clays with satisfaction.

One might hope that Mr. Busack's experience also extended to wilderness survival and frostbite treatment; for at close to six thousand feet, his pottery site qualifies as the highest this country has known! In any case, Busack is said to have turned out jugs, jars, platters, and flowerpots, including large ornamental terra-cotta jardinieres.

The earthenware industry of Utah was of much greater dimension than that of its sister states, primarily because of the isolation of its Mormon inhabitants, who were for some years in a state of virtual warfare with the United States government and the inhabitants of surrounding territories.

Cut off from the sources supplying industrial ceramics, they were forced to rely upon redware in much the same manner as country folk of the eighteenth and early nineteenth century. In fact, Utah's earliest known potter, Heber Chase Kimball, had been trained at his brother Charles's small earthenware kiln near Mendon, New York, in the 1820s. Converted to the Mormon faith, he followed Brigham Young west to Ohio and Illinois, finally reaching Utah in 1847. While Kimball became a ranking member of the church hierarchy, others took over the job of producing ware for the growing settlements.

By 1875, no less than fifteen potters were at work in the Salt Lake City–Provo area. A surprising number of these were Scandanavian converts, particularly Danes, whose lead-glazed redware milk pans, bowls, and jars bore a remarkable resemblance to Early American forms.

Among these immigrant craftsmen was Nielse Jensen, active in Salt Lake City c. 1850–60. Another early worker in the same community was Frederick Petersen, whose kiln, built in 1852, remained in operation until at least 1875. By that time Salt Lake City could boast of several other manufactories, including those run by the Eardley brothers, Bedsen, James, and John, and of William and Benjamin Blake. Both these family businesses date to the 1860s and 1870s.

John Eardley was also the operator of another pioneer pottery, this one located at St. George, in the very southwestern corner of the state.

Established in 1853 and still going strong in 1880, it was one of the longest-lasting Utah concerns. Likewise, far distant from Salt Lake City were the shops of Ephraim Roberts at Vernal near the Colorado border, in business c. 1865–80; and Ralph M. Rowley in Fillmore, about midway down the present Route 15 from Salt Lake City to St. George. Rowley is known to have worked from 1860 to about 1870.

The majority of the Mormon potteries were, however, located in the fertile valley stretching north from Provo to Hyrum near the Utah border. Peter Roberts established the first Provo works around 1860. By 1871 this manufactory, known as the City Pottery, was under the management of A. H. Bowen, who continued it into the 1880s. In the meantime, two of Bowen's former employees, the Danish brothers August and E. C. Henrichsen, built their own pottery in 1872, operating the business well into the twentieth century. Still one more Provo firm was the Zion Cooperative Pottery run by William D. Roberts and also active during the 1870s.

Frederick F. Hansen, yet another Dane, built the first kiln in Brigham City. Born in Copenhagen in 1833, Hansen migrated to the United States at nineteen years of age, arriving as both a Mormon convert and an apprentice to the master potter Nielse Jensen of Salt Lake City. Hansen stayed with Jensen from 1852 until 1854, when he went north to Brigham City and built an adobe house and kiln on First Street.

After nearly twenty years of independence, Hansen was asked to establish a church-sponsored cooperative factory. He undertook this task in 1874, pursuing his labors until the venture was discontinued. Like many other former potters, he then became a farmer, an occupation he pursued until his death in 1901.

The pottery at Hyrum, just south of Logan, Utah, was run by James J. Hansen, believed to be a relative of Frederick. Another long-lived business, it remained in operation from 1856 until 1909. A substantial quantity of redware, including bulbous cream pots and beautifully formed plates, is attributed to this kiln.

CALIFORNIA AND OREGON

The Spanish are known to have made earthenware in San Francisco before 1800, but it was not until a half-century later that the industry was established on a firm basis. East Oakland, across the bay, became the center, with three manufactories: Daniel Brannon's, Pioneer Pottery (c. 1856–87); the California Pottery of Miller and Winsor, active from 1875 until 1900; and the East Oakland Pottery (c. 1870–80). All

Redware cream pot slipped in an orangish white and made and marked by Cyrus Cornell, East Aurora, N.Y., c. 1835–42. This form is much more often found in stoneware. ▶

three made redware, mostly in the form of flowerpots and ornamental terra-cotta. The Brannon shop also produced yellow ware and stoneware.

The California Pottery was a true pioneer enterprise. Begun by the Scottish potter James Miller, the works at first consisted of a single room, but by 1887 it had grown to encompass three kilns and numerous accessory structures. Miller's plant was still functioning at the turn of

Ohio mixing bowls, c. 1900–30. Left, made and marked by Weller Pottery, Zanesville, Ohio; right, unmarked but probably Zanesville.

the century, then being known as the Oakland Art Pottery and Terra Cotta Works.

Terra Cotta, California, a settlement ninety miles from San Diego, promised at one point to become the flowerpot capital of the West. However, after reaching a high point in the 1880s and 1890s Terra Cotta quietly expired, leaving Los Angeles as the major producer of red earthenwares in the southern portion of the state. Large quantities of useful items, primarily flowerpots, were made in Los Angeles, particularly by the firm of J. A. Bauer & Company, active c. 1890–1958. Though Bauer made both yellow ware and stoneware, the firm also produced utilitarian vessels in redware. Several marked bowls and storage pots are known. Another Los Angeles concern that made redware was Gladding, McBean & Company (c. 1875–1945).

Oregon appears to have had but a single redware kiln, that of S. H. Way, active at Eola, a few miles west of Salem, between 1863 and 1869. Way was more than a potter, he was an innovator, though not a particularly successful one, judging from the brief life of his pottery. In 1868, the *Salem Daily Record* visited Way's premises, noting that the proprietor was "such a man as the country is at this time most in need of. He is a great experimenter. He has discovered a kind of ochre, and also a kind of material which will answer the purpose of glazing."

Apparently, such ingenuity was not enough. Way was succeeded at Eola by William Ramsey, Jr., who is believed to have made little if any redware, concentrating his attention on the stoneware he would later produce at Buena Vista.

MARKS OF AMERICAN
REDWARE POTTERS

UNLIKE STONEWARE MANUFACTURERS, most of whom marked at least some of their wares, redware potters seldom identified their products. This was because, due to its fragile nature, redware was customarily sold either at the kiln or within a few miles of it; in these places the local potter would be well known. Nevertheless, a substantial number of marked examples have been identified. The following list, while hardly complete, should provide the collector with information sufficient to recognize most of the marked redware on the market. All marks are printed exactly as observed on existent pieces; and, unless otherwise noted, are impressed. Slashes within a mark indicate the end of a line.

Alld, John; Biddeford, Me., c. 1811–65; J.ALLD/ 1811 (incised in script).

Andrews, Thomas; Chatham County, N.C., c. 1774–79. T H ANDREWS (incised in script).

Aust, Gottfried; Salem, N.C., c. 1771–88; GOTTFRIED AUST ANNO 1773 (slip script).

Bacher, Abraham; Pa., c. 1860–65; ABRAHAM BACHER (incised in script).

Bacher (Baecher), Anthony W.; Bonaughton Township, Pa., Thurmont, Md., and Winchester, Va., c. 1849–89; ANTHONY W. BACHER (incised in script), A.W. BACHER (incised in script), ANTHONY BACHER/WINCHESTER (incised in script), BAECHER (incised in script), BAECHER/ WINCHESTER (incised in script), BAECHER/WINCHESTER, VA. (incised in script), A.W. BAECHER/ WINCHESTER, VA. (incised in script), BACHER.

Bastian, Jacob; Milton, Pa., c. 1823–58; JACOB/ BASTIAN/MILTON/1858 (slip script).

Bayley, William; Newburyport, Mass., c. 1786–99; W.B. (slip script).

Bell, John; Winchester, Va., Chambersburg and Waynesboro, Pa., c. 1827–80; J.BELL, JOHN BELL, JOHN BELL/WAYNESBORO.

Base of a large redware milk pan impressed HOWE & CO *and attributed to Thomas Howe, Athens, N.Y., c. 1805–13. Only a few potters marked their wares on the base, the shoulder being the preferred place.*

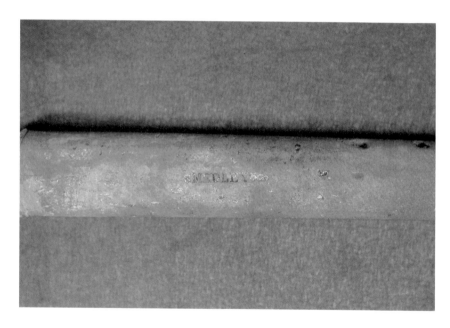

Detail of an individual redware candle mold made and marked by Enos Smedley of Chester County, Pa., c. 1820–56. Marked candle molds are quite uncommon.

Bell, John W.; Waynesboro, Pa., c. 1880–95; JOHN W. BELL/WAYNESBORO, PA.

Bell, Nathan C.; Cornwall, N.Y., c. 1834–40; NATHAN C. BELL, CORNWALL, N.Y.

Bell, Peter; Winchester, Va., c. 1824–45; P.BELL.

Bell, Samuel; Winchester and Strasburg, Va., c. 1824–50; S.BELL.

Bell, Samuel and Solomon; Strasburg, Va., c. 1837–82; SOLOMON BELL, SOLOMON BELL (incised in script), SOLOMON BELL/STRASBURG, SOLOMON BELL/STRASBURG, VA.

Bell, Solomon; Winchester, Va., c. 1830–37; SOLOMON BELL/WINCHESTER (incised in script).

Bell, Upton; Waynesboro, Pa., c. 1895–99; UPTON BELL/WAYNESBORO or UPTON BELL/ WAYNESBORO, PA.

Bixler, Absalom; Lancaster County, Pa., c.

1820–84; ABSALOM BIXLER. TO HIS WIFE SARAH. 1824 or ABS BIXLER (both incised in script).

Blaney, Justus; Cookstown, Pa., c. 1825–54; JUSTUS BLANEY; J.L. BLANEY.

Bodge, Moulton; Fayette, Me., c. 1823–50; MB (incised in script).

Brooks, Hervey; Goshen, Ct., c. 1814–64; H.BROOKS or H.B. 1858, H.B. 1862 (both in slip script).

Buttner, John; Bethabara, N.C., c. 1802–19; J.BUTTNER (incised in script).

Caire, Jacob; Poughkeepsie, N.Y., c. 1845–48; JACOB CAIRE POKEEPSIE.

Caire, John B.; Poughkeepsie, N.Y., c. 1845–52; J.B. CAIRE & CO./PO'KEEPSIE/N.Y. (rare molded flask).

Carey, John; Shippensburg, Pa., c. 1817–50; J. CAREY; J.CAREY & CO.

Clark, Daniel; Lyndeboro, N.H., c. 1792; MADE BY DANIEL CLARK IN LYNDEBOROUGH DURING THE YEAR 1792 (incised in script).

Cope, Darlington; Chester County, Pa., c. 1831–55; D.COPE.

Cornell, Elija; DeRuyter, N.Y., c. 1824–41; E.C. (incised in script).

Crafts, Thomas; Whately, Mass., c. 1806–48; T.CRAFTS.

Crolius, Clarkson, Jr.; New York, N.Y., c. 1835–49; C.CROLIUS/MANUFACTURER/NEW YORK (on unique Albany slip–glazed redware jug).

Dailey, Samuel; Elizabethtown, Pa., c. 1852–72; S.L. DAILEY.

Day, Absalom; Norwalk, Ct., c. 1796–1834; DAYS POTTERY (slip script).

Dodge, Benjamin; Portland, Me., c. 1835–75; B.DODGE/PORTLAND.

Drach, Rudolph; Bedminster, Pa., c. 1780–95; RUDOLPH DRACH POTTER IN BEDMINSTER TOWN-SHIP, 1792 (incised in script).

Dry, Daniel; Dryville, Berks County, Pa., c. 1850–80; D.DRY or D.

Dry, John; Dryville, Berks County, Pa., c. 1804–50; D.

Duche, Andrew; Charlestown, S.C., c. 1735–37; AD.

Durell, Phillip; Elizabeth, N.J., c. 1793; MAN-UFACTURED BY/PHILLIP DURELL/OCTOBER 27TH 1793 (slip script).

Eberly, Jacob J.; Strasburg, Va., c. 1880–1906; J.EBERLY & CO./STRASBURG, VA., J.EBERLY & BRO./STRASBURG,VA., FROM/J.EBERLY & BRO., EBERLY & SON/STRASBURG,VA.

Fare, Henry; Tulpehocken Township, Berks County, Pa., c. 1870–85; H.F.

Feeg, Joseph; Womelsdorf, Berks County, Pa., c. 1856–64; J.FEEG.

Fretz, Jacob; Bucks County, Pa., c. 1809–14; JACOB FRETZ or J.FRETZ (both incised in script).

Funck, Jacob; Bucks County, Pa., c. 1804; IACOB FUNCK/1804 (incised in script).

Gantz, Henry; Lancaster, Pa., c. 1842–80; GANTZ/E.ORANGE ST LANC PA.

Gast, Conrad; Lancaster, Pa., c. 1841–92; MARCH 20TH 74/CONRAD GAST (incised in script); C.GAST.

Gast, Henry; Lancaster, Pa., c. 1838–1913; H.GAST, EAGLE PORCELAIN WORKS/LANCASTER CITY PA/HENRY GAST S Q ST.

Gibble, John; Manheim, Pa., c. 1850–56; J.G. (incised in script).

Gleason, Charles; Morganville, N.Y., c. 1845–58; C.GLEASON, C.GLEASON/MORGANVILL.

Gregory, John Betts; Clinton, N.Y., c. 1810–29; MADE/BY/JBG/OCT 18,1823/CLINTON (slip script).

Grier, Ralph J.; Chester County, Pa., c. 1870–1902; R.J.GRIER.

Grimm, Solomon; Berks County, Pa., c. 1815–25; GRIMM (incised in script).

Grindstaff, William; Happy Valley, Tenn., c. 1865–88; W. GRINDSTAFF.

Haig, James and Thomas; Philadelphia, Pa., c. 1831–78; J. & T. HAIG.

Hamlyn, George F.; Bridgeton, N.J., c. 1883–1905; EAST LAKE POTTERY BRIDGETON, N.J.; GEORGE F. HAMLYN/EAST LAKE POTTERY/BRIDGETON/N.J.

Hancock, John and William; South Amboy, N.J., c. 1826–36; HANCOCK POTTERY (slip script).

Haring, David; Nockamixon, Pa., c. 1830–40; DAVID HARING BUCKS COUNTY PENNSYLVAN (incised in script).

Harwick, Joseph; Bucks County, Pa., c. 1832; J X H (incised in script).

Headman, Andrew; Bucks County, Pa., c. 1805–40; AH 1808 or ANDREW HEADMAN (both incised in script).

Headman, Charles; Rockhill, Pa., c. 1840–70; C.H. or CHAS. HEADMAN (incised in script).

Heiser, Henry H. and William S. Maize; Millheim, Pennsylvania, c. 1871–74; H.H. HEISER W.S. MAIZE, MILLHEIM (incised in script).

Hempstead, Austin; Greenport, N.Y., c. 1838–50; A.H.

Hempstead, Austin E.; Flushing, N.Y., c. 1888–90; A.HEMPSTEAD/FLUSHING,L.I.

Henkle, Jesse; Botetourt County, Va., c. 1830–50; JESSE HENKLE BOTETOURT CO VIRGINIA/1839.

Henne, Joseph S.; Upper Tulpehocken Township, Berks County, Pa., c. 1846–62; J.S. HENNE.

Hilfinger, Alexander; Fort Edward, N.Y., c. 1884–1942; HAND MADE/A.HILFINGER/FORT EDWARD, N.Y.; FORT EDWARD, N.Y.

Holland, John Frederic; Salem, N.C., c. 1821–43; HOLLAND (incised in script).

Howe, Thomas and Nathan Clark; Athens, N.Y., c. 1805–13; HOWE & CO.

Hubener, George; Montgomery County, Pa., c. 1785–98; G.H. or THIS DISH IS MADE BY GEORG HUBENER (both incised in script).

Jackson, William; Saugus, Mass., c. 1811–15; JACKSON (incised in script).

James, Aaron; Westtown, Pa., c. 1790–1823; AARON JAMES/1805 (incised in script).

James, Aaron, Jr.; Westtown, Pa., c. 1820–1821; A. JAMES, JR. (incised in script).

Johnson, Lorenzo; Newstead, N.Y., c. 1848–80; L.JOHNSON, L.JOHNSON/NEWSTEAD, L. JOHNSON & CO./NEWSTEAD.

Keller, Samuel; Bucks County, Pa., c. 1814–30; S.K. (incised in script).

Kersey, Jesse; Chester County, Pa., c. 1790–1824; J.KERSEY (incised in script).

Kline, Philip; Carversville, Pa., c. 1809; P X K (incised in script).

Klinker, Christian; Bucksville, Pa., c. 1773–92, C.K (incised in script).

Lewis, Elonzo D.; Bushnell's Basin, N.Y., c. 1848–55; E.D. LEWIS/BUSHNELL'S BASIN.

Link, Christian; Stonetown, Berks County, Pa., c. 1870–1909; C.LINK or C.LINK/EXETER or C.LINK/EXETER/POTTERY.

McCully, Joseph & Sons; Trenton, N.J., c. 1814–68; J.MCCULLY/TRENTON.

Maize, William S.: see Heiser, Henry H.

Mann, John; Rahway, N.J., c. 1830–50; JOHN MANN/RAHWAY, N.J.; JOHN MANN, RAHWAY.

Matthews, Caleb; Gerry, N.Y., c. 1822–50; C.B. & J. MATHEWS/GERRY.

Mehwaldt, Carl; Bergholz, N.Y., c. 1851–87; C.M. BERGHOLZ 1883; CARL MEHWALDT, BERGHOLZ; M (all marks incised in script).

Miller, Solomon; Hampton, Pa., c. 1863–90; MADE BY ME/JUNE 10TH 1899/SOLOMON MILLER (incised in script).

Miller, Solomon; Newport, Perry County, Pa., c. 1838–95; SOLOMON MILLER/JUNE 20/1888 (incised in script); other pieces with name and various dates.

Monday, John; Bucks County, Pa., c. 1828; JOHN MONDAY (incised in script).

Neese, Johannes; Tyler's port, Pa., c. 1800–30; JOHANNES NEESZ AO 1812, J. NEIS, NEISS, JN, or J.N. (all incised in script).

Noll, Anthony, Monroe Township, Snyder County, Pa., c. 1857–59; ANTHONY NOLL/ 1858 or ANTHONY NOLL/SNYDER CO./MAY 2ND/ 1858 (both incised in script).

Obenshane, Peter & Matthew; Fincastle, Botetourt County, Va., c. 1850–80; 1868/MATTHEW/OBENSHANE (incised in script).

Parker, Clement R.; Greenwood Township, Columbia County, Pa., c. 1855–60; MADE BY C.R. PARKER, GREENWOOD, COL. CO. (incised in script).

Parker, Kester; Greenwood Township, Columbia County, Pa., c. 1854–69; K.PARKER/ GREENWOOD/COL CO.

Paulus (Pullis), Cornelius; New York, N.Y., c. 1792–98; C.P. (incised in script).

Purdy, Solomon; Zoar, Tuscarawas County, Ohio, c. 1834–50; S.PURDY/ZOAR or ZOAR.

Ranninger, Conrad; Montgomery County, Pa., c. 1835–45; CONRAD K. RANNINGER, JUNE TH 23, 1838 (incised in script).

Roseberry, William; Warren County, N.J., c. 1879–81; WM ROSEBERRY/SEIGLETOWN, WARREN CO./N.J./FEB 5TH 1879 (incised in script).

Roth, Heinrich; Pa., c. 1804; H.R. 1804 (incised in script).

Rothrock, Friedrich; Friedberg, N.C., c. 1793–1839; F.R.

Roudebuth, Henry; Montgomery County, Pa., c. 1810–25; HENRY ROUDEBUTH or HR (incised in script).

Rudolph, Henry; Shippensburg, Pa., c. 1877; H.RUDOLPH.

Rudolph, Valentine; Shippensburg, Pa., c. 1867–88; V.RUDOLPH.

Safford, John M.; Monmouth, Me., c. 1830–80, JOHN M. SAFFORD/STEW POT NO. 3.

Safford, John M. and Allen; Monmouth, Me., c. 1840–50; SAFFORD & ALLEN/MONMOUTH ME.

Safford, John, II; Monmouth, Me., c. 1822–54; JOHN SAFFORD; JOHN SAFFORD/MONMOUTH; JOHN SAFFORD 2D; JOHN SAFFORD 2ND/MONMOUTH, MAINE.

Samuel Bell & Sons (Richard Franklin Bell and Charles Forest Bell); Strasburg, Va., c. 1882–1908; S.BELL & SONS (incised in script), S.BELL & SONS/STRASBURG; BELL.

Schaffner, Henry; Salem, N.C., c. 1834–76; H.S./SALEM (incised in script).

Seagle, Daniel; Lincoln County, N.C., c. 1819–30; D.S.

Seigle, Jacob; Warren County, N.J., c. 1799–1821; J.SEIGLE (incised in script).

Singer, Simon; Haycock Township, Pa., c. 1850–80; S. SINGER POTTER (slip script) or MADE AT SINGER'S /POTTERY/HAYCOCK (incised in script).

Smedley, Enos; Westtown and West Chester, Pa., c. 1820–54; ENOS SMEDLEY/WESTTOWN/ 1825 (incised in script) or E.SMEDLEY & CO or SMEDLEY & CO.

Smith, Daniel; Greenwood, Columbia County, Pa., c. 1854–59; D.SMITH/GREENWOOD/COLUMBIA CO/PA.

Smith, Joseph; Wrightstown, Pa., c. 1763–99; J. SMITH or SMITH (both incised in script).

Smith, William J.; Bridgeton, N.J., c. 1870–1908; GRANDMOTHER'S PIE DISH/FIRE PROOF/ W.J.SMITH/BRIDGETON, N.J. or WM. SMITH (incised in script).

Smith, Willoughby; Womelsdorf, Pa., c. 1864–1905; W.SMITH/WOMELSDORF or WILLOUGHBY SMITH/WUMELSDORF or W.SMITH/POTTER/JUNE 16/1862 (incised in script).

Snyder, George; Woodward, Pa., c. 1836–61; GS.

Speece, Henry M.; Shippensburg, Pa., c. 1860–73; H.M. SPEECE.

Spigle, Philip; Fincastle, Va., c. 1840–50; S.

Spinner, David; Bucks County, Pa., c. 1801–11; DAVID SPINNER POTTER or DAVID SPINNER

HIS MAKE (both incised in script) or D.SPINNER (slip script).

Stofflet, Heinrich; Berks County, Pa., c. 1814; HEINRICH STOFFLET (incised in script).

Stout, Jacob; Bucks County, Pa., c. 1762–75; J.S. (incised in script).

Strawhen, Thomas; Bucks County, Pa., c. 1793; T.S. (incised in script).

Suter, Emanuel; Harrisonburg, Va., c. 1855–70; E.SUTER.

Swope, Daniel; Lancaster, Pa., c. 1869–92; D.SWOPE & SON/LANCASTER,PA.

Swope, Henry; Mechanicsburg, Lancaster County, Pa., c. 1850–86; HENRY SWOPE S./1851/POTTERY.

Taney, Jacob; Bucks County, Pa., c. 1794; I.T.

Tomlinson, Lewis K.; Dryville Church, Berks County, Pa., c. 1860–86; LKT.

Troxell, Henry; Montgomery County, Pa., c. 1823; H.T. (incised in script).

Troxell, Samuel; Pottstown, Pa., c. 1823–33; S.T., S.T.P. 1824 or SAMUEL TROXEL POTTER (all incised in script).

Uhler, Andrew; Pa., c. 1810; A.U. MARCH 3, 1810 (incised in script).

Utz, Henry; Cumberland Township, Adams County, Pa., c. 1874–83; H.UTZ.

Vickers, Ann T.; Lionville, Pa., c. 1865–74; A.T.V. or V.

Vickers, John; Lionville, Pa., c. 1823–60; JOHN VICKERS & SON LIONVILLE (incised in script).

Vickers, Thomas; East Caln, Pa., c. 1796–1822; VICKERS/1802 (incised in script).

Weaver, Abraham; Bucks County, Pa., c. 1824–47; ABRAHAM WEAVER (incised in script).

Weber, J. A.; Schuylkill, Pa., c. 1870–80; J.A.WEBER.

Whartenby, Alexander B.; Waterloo, N.Y., c. 1857–94; A.WHARTENBY/WATERLOO,N.Y.

Wilcox, Alvin; West Bloomfield, N.Y., c. 1825–62; A.WILCOX or A.WILCOX/W. BLOOMFIELD.

Wilcox, Alvin and Alvin Hurlburt; West Bloomfield, N.Y., c. 1855; A. WILCOX & HURLBURT/WEST BLOOMFIELD or A.WILCOX/G.HURLBURT/WEST BLOOMFIELD.

Wilcox, Alvin and Edwin Prosser; West Bloomfield, N.Y., c. 1850–55; A.WILCOX/ED PROSSER.

Woolford, F.; Farmington, Mo., c. 1840–50; F. WOOLFORD/FARMINGTON MO.

Wright, Franklin T.; Taunton, Mass., c. 1846–66; F.T. WRIGHT & CO./STONEWARE/TAUNTON (found on redware milk pan).

Zigler, Henry; Newville, Pa., c. 1852–63; H.H. ZIGLER/NEWVILLE PA.

GLOSSARY

AS WE ALL are aware, knowledge is power; and vocabulary is often the standard by which others define us. This appendix of commonly used ceramics terms is designed to allow the collector to understand the language of the field and to use that language to let others—dealers, collectors, and auction-house personnel—know that he or she is a knowledgeable participant in the field.

Albany slip: A rich brown slip formed by mixing water with a fine brown clay, first found at Albany, New York, but also mined in California, Michigan, Texas, and other states. It is widely used to glaze stoneware, and sometimes as a redware finish.

Applied decoration: Pottery decoration that is separately molded or hand-formed and then attached, using slip, to a ceramic body prior to firing.

Bisque: Also known as *biscuit*, this occurs when a ceramic body has been fired once but not yet glazed.

Body: A technical term for the combination of clays used in producing a piece of pottery.

Bolts: Elongated, loglike pieces of refined clay ready to be worked or shaped.

Burning: The process of firing pottery in a kiln.

Ceramic: A mineral-based substance, such as earthenware or stoneware, that is fired at a high temperature to a hard state.

Clay: An earth or soil that becomes malleable when wet and hard after firing.

Cobalt oxide: Also called *cobalt*, it is a compound that, when mixed with silica and potash, produces a blue glaze generally used to decorate stoneware and rarely used on redware.

Cockspurs: Three pointed pieces of unglazed, baked clay used to separate pieces of pottery during firing.

Coggle wheel: A small wooden or metal wheel with a shaped rim and handle that is used to make decorative impressions in soft, unbaked clay.

Coleslaw decoration: A form of applied decoration that consists of many tiny convoluted strands of clay that resemble wood shavings. It is found on some Pennsylvania and Virginia redware.

Collar: A thick, raised band encircling the neck of a crock or jar.

Crazing: Tiny cracks in ceramic glazes produced by the differing rates at which the body and glaze contract in cooling after firing or through age; also termed *spidering*.

Delftware: See *Faience*.

Drape molding: The process of shaping a ceramic body by laying slabs of unfired clay over a form, pressing it down, and then trimming off the excess, much as in making a pie crust; it was commonly used in the manufacture of redware pie plates and platters.

Earthenware: Slightly porous pottery that is fired at a relatively low temperature. Redware is a type of earthenware.

Embossing: Raised decoration formed by molding or hand shaping; it is not separately made and then applied.

Engobe: Thin white opaque tin glaze used as base for decoration in faience or delftware as well as some American slip-decorated or sgraffito wares.

Faience: Earthenware, usually redware, covered with an opaque white tin glaze that is then covered with overglaze decoration in other colors.

Finial: A molded or hand-shaped knob or protrusion that serves as the lift or handle on a lid.

Firing: Heating a ceramic body to the desired hardness in a kiln.

Glaze: A mixture of clay, water, sand, and various metallic oxides or alkalies that is applied to a ceramic body before firing; it vitrifies during the firing process, producing a water-resistant surface.

Glaze mill: A device consisting of two stones, the smaller top one rotating against the stationary bottom one, used to grind glaze ingredients to a fine powder before use.

Green ware: Unfired pottery.

Impressed decoration: Ceramic decoration created by pressing a shaped wood or metal stamp into the soft clay surface before firing. See also *Coggle wheel*.

Incised decoration: Ceramic decoration created by a sharp, pointed instrument used to scratch designs into the soft clay body prior to firing. The best examples are seen in Pennsylvania sgraffito ware.

Iron oxide: Red or black oxide of iron used to color lead glazes.

Jack: A form of handpress used in removing foreign bodies from clay prior to use in potting.

Kaolin: A fine clay that fires to a pure white; often employed in Connecticut and Pennsylvania slip-script decoration, where it appears yellow under the overall lead glaze.

Kiln: A stone or brick oven or furnace in which ceramic products are baked.

Lead glaze: A redware glaze consisting of a mixture of lead oxide, water, sand, and clay that fires to a shiny, glasslike surface.

Leather-hard: A term applied to green ware that is still wet but no longer plastic or flexible. Also termed *rubber-hard*.

Lip: See *Rim*.

Majolica: The Italian term for *faience*.

Manganese oxide: A metallic oxide used in ceramic glazes that ranges from purplish brown to black when fired; often employed on red-ware.

Mark: The name, and sometimes the address of a potter, that has been impressed, incised, or ink-stamped on his wares.

Modeling: Shaping a soft clay body by hand and with hand-held tools.

Molding: The process of shaping pottery, either by pouring liquid clay or pressing soft clay into a mold and allowing it to harden there; once removed from the mold the piece retains its form. See also *Press molding*.

Neck: The narrow area between the rim and shoulder of a piece of pottery.

Overglaze decoration: Decoration applied after a piece has been glazed once and fired; a second firing, at a lower temperature, is usually employed to "set" this decoration.

Paste: The clay body from which a piece of pottery is made. See also *Body*.

Pierced decoration: Decoration produced by cutting out areas of a clay body. This technique is often found on early Pennsylvania redware, such as sugar bowls and compotes.

Pipe clay: See *Kaolin*.

Plasticity: That property of a clay body that allows its form to be changed by pressure without cracking, and to retain a new shape when the pressure is removed.

Potter's wheel: A machine on which ceramic objects are shaped. The simplest consists of two disks joined by a shaft and set in a wooden frame; as the lower disk is turned, often by the foot, the upper disk, upon which the clay body rests, rotates.

Pottery: Ceramics made from a clay or a mixture of clays; also the shop or factory where ceramics are manufactured.

Presentation pieces: Pottery intended as a gift or to commemorate a special occasion; often ornate, one-of-a-kind pieces, sometimes with a date and the name or initials of the recipient.

Press molding: The process of shaping pottery bodies in which plastic clay slabs are pressed by hand or a mechanical plunger into plaster or clay molds. See also *Molding*.

Production pieces: Standard wares made by most redware potteries such as jugs, jars, pots, and churns; they are produced in quantity.

Pug Mill: a cylindrical rod in which clay is ground and mixed prior to use.

Quern: See *Glaze mill*.

Redware: Nonvitrified pottery made from clays that fire at a temperature of 1,000 to 1,100° C. to a porous, relatively coarse and brittle body of a light rose-pink to reddish brown hue.

Ribs: Pieces of shaped metal or wood used by the potter to form ware as it turns on the potter's wheel.

Rim: The upper edge of a piece of ceramic ware; also termed the *lip*.

Rouletting: Banded decoration produced by a coggle wheel.

Rubber-hard: See *Leather-hard*.

Setting tiles: oblong slabs of unglazed, baked clay used to separate ware during firing.

Sgraffito: A decorative technique, particularly employed on Pennsylvania redware, in which a potter covers an earthenware body with a coat of opaque slip and then scratches designs through the slip, partially revealing the underlying clay body.

Sherd: Also called *shard*, is a fragment of broken, usually antique, pottery.

Shoulder: That part of a ceramic body between the waist and neck.

Slip: A suspension of ceramic materials in water.

Slip casting: the process of forming ceramic through the use of molds and slip.

Slip cup: A small hollow cuplike device with tubes that are often made from turkey-feather quills or reeds; colored slip is trailed or dribbled through the tubes to create decorative patterns on a ceramic surface.

Slip decoration: Redware decoration composed of colored slip, applied with a slip cup or brush.

Slip script: Slip decoration in the form of initials, names, or expressions, such as "Currant Pie" or "Mary's Dish."

Spidering: See *Crazing*.

Sponged decoration: Redware decoration that consists of colored slip applied at random or in a pattern and with a sponge or cloth. The most typical type is a manganese black decoration on a red clay body.

Sprigging: The application, using slip, of separately molded decorative elements, such as handles or masks, to a leather-hard ceramic body.

Throwing: The process of forming vessels on the potter's wheel; also referred to as *turning*.

Tin glaze: A lead-based glaze that is opaque, due to the presence of tin oxide. See *Faience*.

Turning: See *Throwing*.

Underglaze decoration: Decoration applied to a bisqued ceramic body before the application of a glaze.

Waist: The widest part of a ceramic body.

Wheel-thrown: Shaped by hand on a potter's wheel.

BIBLIOGRAPHY

THE FOLLOWING BOOKS have been selected as helpful to the student of American redware. Some are most valuable for their text, others for the photographs they contain. Many are out of print but can be located through used-book dealers. As is the case with every area of antiques and collectibles, a good reference library is often the key to success.

Barber, Edwin A. *Lead Glazed Pottery*. New York: Doubleday, Page & Co., 1907.

———. *Marks of American Potters*. Philadelphia: Patterson and White Co., 1904. Reprint. Southampton, N.Y.: The Cracker Barrel Press, 1972.

———. *The Pottery & Porcelain of the United States: An Historical Review of American Ceramic Art from the Earliest Times to the Present Day*. New York and London: Putnam's Sons, 1893. Reprint combined with *Marks of Amer-ican Potters*. New York: Feingold & Lewis, 1976.

———. *Tulip Ware of the Pennsylvania-German Potters*. Philadelphia: Pennsylvania Museum, 1926. Reprint. New York: Dover, 1970.

Barons, Richard I. *18th and 19th Century American Folk Pottery*. New Paltz: State University of New York, 1969.

Barret, Richard C. *Bennington Pottery and Porcelain*. New York: Bonanza Books, 1958.

Bivins, John, Jr. *The Moravian Potters in North Carolina*. Chapel Hill: University of North Carolina Press, 1972.

Branin, M. Lelyn. *The Early Makers of Hand-crafted Earthenware and Stoneware in Central and Southern New Jersey*. Rutherford, N.J.: Fairleigh Dickinson University Press, 1988.

———. *The Early Potters and Potteries of Maine*. Middletown, Ct.: Wesleyan University Press, 1978.

Breininger, Lester P., Jr. *Potters of the Tulpe-*

hocken. Robesonia, Pa., 1979 (privately published).

Burrison, John A. *Georgia Jug Makers: A History of Southern Folk Pottery*. Ann Arbor: University Microfilms International, 1973.

Clement, Arthur W. *Our Pioneer Potters*. Brooklyn, N.Y.: Maple Press, 1947.

Conway, Bob, and Ed Gilreath. *Traditional Pottery in North Carolina*. Waynesville, N.C.: The Mountaineer, 1974.

Corbett, Cynthia Arps. *Useful Art: Long Island Pottery*. Setauket, N.Y.: Society for the Preservation of Long Island Antiquities, 1985.

Force, Peter, ed., *Tracts and Other Papers Relating Principally to the Origin, Settlement and Progress of Colonies in North America*. Washington, D.C.: Peter Smith, 1844.

Guilland, Harold F. *Early American Folk Pottery*. Philadelphia: Chilton Books, 1971.

Hillier, Bevis. *Pottery and Porcelain 1700–1914*. Des Moines and New York: Meredith Press, 1968.

Hume, Noel Ivor. *Pottery and Porcelain in Colonial Williamsburg's Archaeological Collections*. Williamsburg, Va.: Colonial Williamsburg Foundation, 1969.

James, Arthur E. *The Potters and Potteries of Chester County, Pennsylvania*. West Chester, Pa.: Chester County Historical Society, 1945. 2ed. Exton, Pa.: Schiffer Publishing Ltd., 1978.

Ketchum, William C., Jr. *Early Potters and Potteries of New York State*. New York: Funk and Wagnalls, 1970. Retitled rev. 2ed. *Potters and Potteries of New York State, 1650–1900*. Syracuse, N.Y.: Syracuse University Press, 1987.

———. *The Knopf Collectors' Guides to American Antiques: Pottery & Porcelain*. New York: Alfred A. Knopf, 1983.

———. *The Pottery and Porcelain Collector's Handbook*. New York: Funk and Wagnalls, 1971.

———. *The Pottery of the State*. Exhibition catalog. New York: Museum of American Folk Art, 1974.

Lasansky, Jeanette. *Central Pennsylvania Redware Pottery: 1780–1904*. Lewisburg, Pa.: The Union County Oral Traditions Projects, 1979.

New Jersey State Museum. *Early Arts of New Jersey: The Potter's Art c. 1680–1900*. Trenton: New Jersey State Museum, 1956.

Perry, Barbara, ed. *American Ceramics: The Collection of the Everson Museum of Art*. New York: Rizzoli International Publications, 1989.

Powell, Elizabeth A. *Pennsylvania Pottery, Tools and Processes*. Doylestown, Pa.: The Bucks County Historical Society, 1972.

Quimby, Ian M. G., ed. *Ceramics in America*. Charlottesville, Va.: University of Virginia Press, 1973.

Ramsay, John. *American Potters and Pottery*. Boston: Hale, Cushman and Flint, 1939. Reprint. New York: Tudor Publishing Co., 1947.

Rice, A. H., and John Baer Stoudt. *The Shenandoah Pottery*. Strasburg, Va.: Shenandoah Publishing House, 1929.

Rochester Museum and Science Center. *Clay in the Hands of the Potter*. Rochester, N.Y.: Rochester House of Printing, 1974.

Schwartz, Marvin D. *Collector's Guide to Antique American Ceramics*. Garden City, N.Y.: Doubleday, 1969.

Smith, Joseph J., with introduction by William C. Ketchum, Jr. *Regional Aspects of American Folk Pottery*. York, Pa.: Historical Society of York County, 1974.

Spargo, John. *Early American Pottery and China*. New York and London: The Century Co., 1926. Reprint. Rutland, Vt.: Charles E. Tuttle, 1974.

————. *The Potters and Potteries of Bennington*. Boston: Houghton Mifflin, 1926. Reprint. New York: Dover, 1972.

Stiles, Helen E. *Pottery in the United States*. New York: E. P. Dutton, 1921.

Stradling, Diana, and J. Garrison, eds. *The Art of the Potter*. Antiques Magazine Library. New York: Universe Books, 1977.

Sudbury, Byron. *Historic Clay Tobacco Pipe Makers in the United States of America*. Oxford, Eng.: BAR International Series, 1979.

Watkins, Laura Woodside. *Early New England Potters and Their Wares*. Cambridge, Mass.: Harvard University Press, 1950. Reprint. Hamden, Ct.: Archon Books, 1968.

Willett, E. Henry, and Joey Brackner. *The Traditional Pottery of Alabama*. Exhibition catalog. Montgomery, Ala.: Montgomery Museum of Fine Arts, 1983.

Wiltshire, William E., III. *Folk Pottery of the Shenandoah Valley*. New York: E. P. Dutton, 1975.

Winton, Andrew L., and Kate B. Winton. *Norwalk Potteries*. Canaan, N.H.: Phoenix Publishing, 1981.

INDEX

Numbers in italics refer to an illustration and its caption

PICTURE CREDITS

Illustrations in this book are from the following public and private collections. Absence of a credit indicates that the owner of the object wishes to remain anonymous.

Author's collection: 33, 35, 37, 66, 70, 74, 75 (right), 77 (bottom), 85

Edward Burak: 39, 91

Clinton, New York, Historical Society: 73 (bottom)

Lillian Blankley Cogan: 42 (top)

Fran and Douglas Faulkner: 51, 122

Mr. and Mrs. George Hammell: 9, 12, 13, 31, 36 (top), 67 (bottom), 69, 72, 73 (top), 75 (left), 77 (top), 87, 102, 103 (bottom), 111 (top), 112, 114, 116, 123, 126

Samuel Herrup: 17, 47, 63, 64, 89

Sharon W. Joel: 26 (bottom), 34, 40, 97 (top), 98

Museum of American Folk Art: 10 (bottom)

George E. Schoellkopf: 26 (bottom), 41, 97 (bottom), 99, 105 (right)

Philadelphia Museum of Art: 82 (top)

Chris Woods: 5 (bottom)